NOTES

including
- *Life and Background of the Author*
- *Introduction to the Novel*
- *List of Characters*
- *Critical Commentaries*
- *Glossaries*
- *Genealogy Chart*
- *Maps*
- *Circular Journey Diagram*
- *Critical Essays*
    Pueblo Ceremonies
    The Peyote Way
    Navajo Chants
    Witchcraft
    Federal Relocation Policy
    Varieties of Narrative Strategy
- *Topics for Discussion and Writing*
- *Selected Bibliography*

by
H. Jaskoski, Ph.D.
California State University Fullerton

INCORPORATED
LINCOLN, NEBRASKA 68501

Editor

Gary Carey, M.A.
University of Colorado

Consulting Editor

James L. Roberts, Ph.D.
Department of English
University of Nebraska

ISBN 0-8220-0597-2
© Copyright 1994
by
Cliffs Notes, Inc.
All Rights Reserved
Printed in U.S.A.

1995 Printing

Cliffs Notes, Inc.   Lincoln, Nebraska

CONTENTS

Centerspread: Genealogy Chart

HOUSE MADE OF DAWN

Notes

LIFE AND BACKGROUND OF THE AUTHOR

In keeping with Kiowa and other Native traditions which see each individual as part of a complex set of kinship, clan, and place relations, N. Scott Momaday opens his memoir, *The Names*, with a long exploration of his ancestry and genealogy. The forebears of his mother, Natachee Scott Momaday, include a Revolutionary War general and a governor of Kentucky, as well as a Cherokee great-grandmother. As a young woman, Natachee Scott determined to reclaim her Native heritage and enrolled at Haskell Institute, an Indian boarding school operated by the federal government through the Bureau of Indian Affairs (BIA). Her son, Navarre Scott Momaday, expresses profound admiration for his mother's decision to identify as Indian, calling it an act of imagination by which she claimed essential identity and meaning. This concept of self-definition is frequently expressed in Momaday's writings and speeches: a person defines himself, he maintains, by imagining himself, and Momaday opens his own memoir with the announcement that the book is an act of the imagination.

Momaday's father, Alfred Momaday, belonged to a distinguished Kiowa family in Oklahoma. One great-great-grandmother was descended from a young woman captured by the Kiowas. Momaday's paternal grandmother, Aho, with whom he spent many childhood hours, and his paternal grandfather, Mammedaty, are central to the poetic evocation of Kiowa tradition and history in another autobiographical work, *The Way to Rainy Mountain*.

In *The Names*, Momaday describes how, some months after his birth in February 1934, he was solemnly given the Kiowa name

Tsoai-talee (Rock-Tree Boy) by Pohd-lohk, his step-grandfather. The name refers to the strange, upthrusting rock formation in Wyoming known as Devil's Tower. It is a highly significant name for Momaday, and he has retold in numerous places the traditional story of the formation of that geological feature of the landscape. The story, which is also related in *House Made of Dawn*, tells how a boy was transformed into a bear; bears have enormous personal significance for the author, and he often uses them as a theme in his writings.

Shortly after Momaday was born, the family—mother, father, and young Scott—moved from Oklahoma to New Mexico. From 1936 to 1943, the family lived in various places on the Navajo reservation: Shiprock, New Mexico, and Tuba City and Chinle, Arizona. Although there were stays in Oklahoma, Kentucky, and Louisiana, the reservations of the Southwest were home. In 1943, World War II provided new employment opportunities for Momaday's parents, and the family spent three years near the army air base at Hobbs, New Mexico, before moving in 1946 to the pueblo of Jemez, New Mexico. Momaday recalls that in Hobbs he encountered ideas of race and acts of racial discrimination: the town included a "niggertown," and he was singled out by young neighbors as a "Jap." Momaday states that people have frequently assumed that he is of Asian descent, an identification that he embraces in his meditation on theories of ancient migrations over the Bering land bridge.

In Jemez, Momaday's parents taught in the day school. He writes with lyric nostalgia of his time at Jemez, where he lived until his last year of high school. Although an outsider in Pueblo culture, he was drawn to the serene rhythms of the corn-growing and sheep-herding society and the deep spiritual beauty of Pueblo life. It was here that Momaday developed an intense aesthetic appreciation for the Navajo people: the Navajo, he has said, "know how to be beautiful." The magnificent landscape of northern New Mexico inspired him, and he spent many hours on horseback exploring the mesas, canyons, and valleys. "Sense of place" and "land ethic" are phrases that recur in Momaday's writing. A constant perception of the integral relationship of the individual to a particular landscape permeates his work.

Momaday's final year of high school was spent at August Military School in Virginia, from which he graduated in 1952. Studies occupied the next eleven years. Momaday graduated from the University of New Mexico in 1958 and briefly attended Virginia Law School. Then, following a year of teaching at Dulce, New Mexico, on the Apache reservation, he entered Stanford University as a creative writing fellow. This was a significant event in his life; at Stanford, his mentor and subsequent close friend was Yvor Winters, a renowned poet and critic who was deeply appreciative (although also critical) of the French Symbolist poets and the American Romantic writers who inspired them. Momaday's doctoral dissertation at Stanford was a definitive edition of the poetry of an American Romantic, Frederick Goddard Tuckerman. Later, he spent a year studying the manuscripts of Emily Dickinson. Much of Momaday's poetry and prose reflect the qualities of Romantic and Symbolist work—a sense of ineffable reality beyond words, a delight in deeply sensuous imagery, especially of nature, and a contemplative approach, characterized by wonder and awe towards reality. Yvor Winters was also one of the people who encouraged Momaday to explore his family's history.

Momaday received his Ph.D. degree in 1963, and in the following years, while producing his major writings, he taught at the University of California in Santa Barbara and Berkeley, at Stanford, at New Mexico State University, and at the University of Arizona. Interrupting his years of teaching at American universities, Momaday spent several months in Moscow in 1975 as the first Fulbright lecturer in American literature in the Soviet Union.

Two events in the 1960s were significant in Momaday's relationship with his Kiowa ancestry: his journey retracing the ancient Kiowa migration from the northern Rockies through the Great Plains, and his initiation into the Gourd Dance Society, a traditional Kiowa religious society. In 1965, after the death of his paternal grandmother, Momaday made the journey north from Oklahoma to South Dakota that was to inspire the Tosamah section of *House Made of Dawn* and be elaborated more fully in the lyrical prose volume, *The Way to Rainy Mountain* (1969). *House Made of Dawn* is Momaday's first published novel, appearing in 1968; the book was acclaimed for its poetry and sensitivity, and it was awarded the Pulitzer Prize for fiction. Other major works are his collection of poems, *The Gourd Dancer* (1976), an autobiographical memoir titled *The Names* (1976), another novel, *The Ancient Child* (1990), and a compilation of out-of-print and new poems and short prose pieces,

In the Presence of the Sun: Stories and Poems, 1961–1991 (1992). In addition to his books, Momaday has published widely in periodicals and anthologies. One of the projects that he recalls with particular pleasure is a regular column he wrote in the 1970s for the New Mexico newspaper *Viva.*

Between the publication of *The Names* in 1976 and the appearance of *The Ancient Child* in 1990, Momaday was in much demand as a lecturer and interview subject. During this time, he published several important essays, including an introduction to American Indian literature for a literary history of the United States. He also worked intensively on another interest, graphic arts, exhibiting prints, drawings, and paintings in several shows. Momaday's interest in graphic arts is reflected in the poetic descriptiveness that suffuses his fiction and other prose, and his use of text in paintings and prints continues his mixing of media, which began with the illustrations by Al Momaday for *The Way To Rainy Mountain* and the author's own illustrations for *The Gourd Dancer* and *The Names.* His latest book, *In the Presence of the Sun: Stories and Poems, 1961–1991,* includes reproductions of many of his prints and drawings.

While rejecting the label "spokesman," Momaday has always been generous and supportive of initiatives for American Indian education and recognition in the arts. One of his earliest publications was an essay in *Ramparts* magazine titled "The Morality of Indian Hating"; appearing at the height of the civil rights struggle, the article brought to the attention of readers the unexplored riches of Indian heritage. He is a compelling speaker and has lectured in prestigious forums; he also makes himself available to chat with a student who wishes to interview him or to make a personal appearance in classes of young students entering university from the reservation. He has supported the work of many young American Indian authors, writing introductions and reviews in order for their names to become better known to the reading public. Momaday is one of the most interviewed of contemporary authors, and tapes and transcripts of these interviews provide much in the way of personal insight into his work.

Today, Momaday is a Distinguished Professor at the University of Arizona and lives in Tucson with his family. He continues a life dedicated to the arts—poetry, prose, visual arts, and storytelling.

INTRODUCTION TO THE NOVEL

The action of *House Made of Dawn* takes place between July 20, 1945 and February 28, 1952. The narration comprises an undated prologue and four dated sections set in the pueblo of Walatowa (Jemez), New Mexico (prologue and sections 1 and 4) and the Los Angeles area (sections 2 and 3).

After a brief prologue describing a man named Abel, who is running in the Southwestern countryside, the story proper opens on July 20, 1945, when Abel, an orphan raised by his traditionalist grandfather, Francisco, returns to Walatowa after serving in World War II. Alienated and disorganized by war experiences (and also, it is suggested, by the early loss of mother and brother and from bouts of malaise), Abel is unable to make a meaningful reintegration into the life of the village.

He takes a temporary job cutting wood for Angela St. John, a troubled, sensuous woman who is visiting the area to undertake mineral bath treatments for some sort of chronic fatigue; she is pregnant. Abel has a brief affair with Angela. He also participates in a village festival and is singled out by a strange, ominous-appearing albino man. Meanwhile, the omniscient narration follows a parallel line with the village priest, Father Olguin, as he studies the diary of his predecessor, Fray Nicolás, and makes an awkward approach to Angela.

On August 1, in a strange, almost ritualistic encounter, Abel stabs the albino to death in a cornfield. This section of the story ends the next day, with Francisco again alone, hoeing in his fields.

The two chapters of the second section are dated January 27 and 28, 1952. This portion of the story takes place in Los Angeles and centers on the character of John Big Bluff Tosamah, who is a Kiowa, a storefront preacher, and a priest of the peyote religion. The chapter for January 27 contains the first of two sermons by Tosamah, a long discourse on a verse from the Gospel of John: "In the beginning was the Word." Tosamah maintains that language has been debased by white people and its power lost or corrupted. At the time that Tosamah is giving this sermon, Abel appears to be lying fifteen miles away, barely conscious after having suffered a terrible beating that has mangled his hands.

The omniscient narrator moves back and forth in time, interspersing fragmentary memories of Abel's past with awareness of his pain-wracked body; he fleetingly recalls filling out forms in prison and, afterwards, meeting an earnest social worker named Milly (with whom he has an affair); there are fragments from his time in prison and testimony at his trial by Father Olguin and by one of his buddies in the army. This chapter also contains a depiction of a peyote ceremony and introduces Ben Benally, who will play a significant part in Abel's eventual healing.

The January 28 chapter is composed almost entirely of Tosamah's second sermon. This is a passage previously published in an essay in *Ramparts* magazine and later in *The Way To Rainy Mountain*, in which Momaday meditates on his Kiowa grandmother's life and the history and passing of the magnificent Kiowa culture.

The third section of the novel is dated February 20, 1952, and is narrated by Ben Benally, a Navajo relocated to urban Los Angeles. Benally's rambling narration includes references to more of Abel's life in Los Angeles—his job at a box-stapling factory, his encounters with a sadistic policeman named Martinez, his participation in the peyote services, and socializing with Milly. Benally also recollects the recent encounter with Angela St. John, who visited Abel in the hospital when he was recovering from the brutal beating that left his hands broken. Angela, now the mother of a son, told Abel a story with a heroic theme, intimating that he reminded her of the hero. Benally also recollects going with Abel to a "49" party in the hills outside the city on the night before Abel was to leave; Benally recalls that at this time, as previously, Abel sang traditional songs from Navajo healing ceremonies, including the verses beginning "House Made of Dawn" from the Night Chant.

The fourth section of *House Made of Dawn* is very brief, containing only two chapters, dated February 27 and February 28, 1952. Abel returns to Walatowa in time to care for his dying grandfather and perform the appropriate burial rituals. Having seen to this duty, he begins a ceremonial run into the dawn. The novel has moved in a circle, returning to the event depicted in the prologue.

LIST OF CHARACTERS

Relatively few characters are involved in the actual events that take place during the time period covered by the novel, between July 1945 and February 1952. Many other characters are mentioned or remembered, often only in a phrase or a single sentence. These secondary, or remembered, characters are noted in a separate list after the list of main characters.

CHARACTERS IN THE NOVEL

Abel

The central character of the novel, born in 1920 of a Walatowa mother and an unknown father. Raised by his grandfather after the death of his mother, he leaves the pueblo of Walatowa to join the army during World War II. His return to the pueblo after getting out of the army begins the novel; his second return ends it.

Francisco

Grandfather of Abel and an elder in the village of Walatowa, Francisco is a mediating figure; he maintains the traditional Indian customs but is sacristan to the Catholic priest. He is a supremely religious, conservative man.

Father Olguin

Parish priest at Walatowa, he feels keenly his alienation as an outsider in the village, and he is fascinated by the diary of a predecessor at the church.

Bonifacio

A young boy who serves as an altar boy for Father Olguin.

Angela Grace (Mrs. Martin) St. John

A woman from Los Angeles who visits Walatowa in the early stages of her pregnancy, on the advice of her physician husband, to seek treatment at the mineral baths for a nervous condition. She becomes Abel's lover. Seven years later, she visits Abel in Los Angeles at the hospital where he is recovering from a beating, and she tells him a story about a bear.

Juan Reyes Fragua

The albino man whom Abel murders.

John Big Bluff Tosamah

Called Priest of the Sun and titled Right Reverend John Big Bluff Tosamah, he ministers to a congregation of displaced Indians in the inner city of Los Angeles. He is a Kiowa with roots in Oklahoma. The pun in his middle names, Big Bluff, suggests his character as a trickster and verbal manipulator.

Cristobal Cruz

One of the disciples of Tosamah. The word *cruz* means "cross" in Spanish.

Ben Benally

A Navajo transplanted from the reservation in northern Arizona to the inner city of Los Angeles, Benally is Abel's mentor, friend, and co-worker; he sings fragments of Navajo ceremonies to cure Abel of his illness. Benally narrates the third of the four main sections of the novel.

Milly

A social worker in Los Angeles who befriends Abel and Benally and has an affair with Abel. Milly's family, like the families she helps, was poor and victimized.

Napoleon Kills-in-the-Timber

One of the participants in the peyote ceremony.

Henry Yellowbull

One of the participants in the peyote ceremony.

REMEMBERED CHARACTERS

Henry

Owner of a bar in Los Angeles.

Martinez

A cruel, corrupt police officer in Los Angeles.

Manygoats

A man whom Benally asks for repayment of a loan. "Manygoats" is a well-known Navajo clan name.

Howard

A friend whom Benally meets in the bar after seeing Abel off on the train.

Carlozini

An old woman living in the apartment below the one shared by Benally and Abel.

Mercedes Tenorio

A woman who starts a stomp dance at the "49."

Daniels

Supervisor at the carton factory where Benally and Abel work.

Peter

The son of Angela Grace St. John.

Vidal

Abel's elder brother, who died when Abel was a young child.

Mariano

Francisco recalls besting Mariano in a race many years before the time of the novel.

Nicolás teah-whau

A woman from Abel's childhood whom children believed was a witch.

Abel's mother

She died when Abel was a very young child.

Juliano Medina

A man of the Sia pueblo who took part with Abel and his grandfather in a ceremony during Abel's youth.

Patiestewa

Head of the Bahkyush Eagle Watchers Society, one of the societies responsible for maintaining the religious ceremonies of Walatowa.

John Raymond

A rancher mentioned in passing; Abel was returning from breaking a horse for him when he saw the awe-inspiring sight of the mating eagles.

San Juanito

The man who caught the old eagle during the eagle hunt in Abel's youth.

Fray Nicolás

A priest at Jemez during the late 1800s; Father Olguin reads his diary, which contains comments on Abel's forebears.

Viviano

A boy mentioned in Fray Nicolás' diary, said to be a brother of Francisco, Abel's grandfather.

Tomacita Fragua

Tomacita is a woman mentioned in Fray Nicolás' diary.

Antonio and Carlos

Mentioned in Fray Nicolás' diary; two men who help bury Tomacita Fragua.

Juan Chinana

Mentioned by Fray Nicolás as his sacristan.

Inocencia, San Juanito, Avelino, Pasqual, Lupita, Augustin

Mentioned in Fray Nicolás' diary as having taken part in a living crèche, a Nativity representation, at Christmas, 1874.

Domingo Gachupin

Mentioned in Fray Nicolás' diary as having taken care of a statue of the Infant of Prague between Christmas and the feast of the Epiphany (6 January).

Avenicio Lucero and Jesus Baca

Mentioned in Fray Nicolás' journal as having died.

Maria Delgado

Mentioned in Fray Nicolás' journal.

Manuelita and Diego Fragua

Mentioned in Fray Nicolás' journal as parents of the albino baby. The diary refers to Diego as the son-in-law of Tomacita Fragua.

Catherine

Sister-in-law of Fray Nicolás, mentioned in his letter to his brother, J.M.

Porcingula Pecos

Mentioned in Fray Nicolás' diary as being impregnated by Francisco—therefore, possibly Abel's grandmother.

John

Youngest of the four evangelists and author of the last of the four Gospels. His name is linked with Tosamah (John Big Bluff) and Angela (St. John).

Fat Josie

Abel remembers how she snapped his back into alignment after a fall from a horse.

Bowker

A soldier whom Abel remembers as testifying during the trial about Abel's bravery under fire.

Corporal Rate and Private Marshall

Soldiers who figure in Bowker's story of Abel's courage.

Daley Fletcher

In Milly's story, the neighbor who drives her to the train when she leaves home.

Matt

Milly's ex-husband.

Carrie

Milly's daughter, who died at a young age of a mysterious fever.

Mr. Hitchcock

In Milly's story, the druggist whom she goes to for help for her child.

Aho

Grandmother of Tosamah.

DeBenedictus

A workman in the carton factory who had been laid off before Abel applied for a job.

Frazer

The manager of a trading post whom Benally remembers from his childhood.

Sam Charley

A friend whom Benally recalls from his youth.

CRITICAL COMMENTARIES

PROLOGUE

The prologue opens the book with a scene-painting passage which describes in three paragraphs the vision of a man named Abel, running in a vast landscape. Like other descriptive passages in the novel, this one is in present tense, emphasizing the timeless beauty of the land and the ageless customs of the people who have lived on it for centuries. It is winter on the high plateau of the Southwest. The man who is running is named Abel, and he has rubbed charcoal and ash on his body according to the custom of the Pueblo people in this area; his running is a ceremonial act, part of a religious observance.

(Here and in the following sections, difficult words, phrases, and colloquialisms are translated for you, as are these below.)

- *Dypaloh*   the opening formula for storytelling in Jemez (the phrase "Once upon a time" is such a formula in English). When the audience hears this word, they know that what follows will be a story.

- **mesquite**   a hardwood tree native to the Southwestern desert; mesquite beans have long been an important source of food for indigenous people.

- *pueblo*   the Spanish word for "settlement," or "town." People lived in these city-states of the Southwest for hundreds of years, in contrast to more nomadic peoples like the Navajos, Apaches, and Utes. Called "Pueblo" Indians by the Spanish settlers, they are considered as a defined cultural group today.

PART 1: THE LONGHAIR

WALATOWA, CAÑON DE SAN DIEGO, 1945

"Longhair" could describe Francisco, grandfather of Abel, the novel's protagonist. Francisco is an elder of the village. The word "Longhair" can also refer to an American Indian man who maintains the old ways, a cultural conservative who does not adopt the modern practice of cutting his hair; it can also indicate a man who has not been educated in the boarding schools operated by the Bureau of Indian Affairs, which used to force Indian boys to cut their hair.

The first and last of the four dated sections of the novel take place in and near Jemez pueblo, one of several Pueblo Indian communities in the Rio Grande Valley of New Mexico. The people of Jemez call their pueblo Walatowa. Place names in the Southwest reflect the region's multicultural character: Jemez and Walatowa are two names for the same pueblo; Cañon de San Diego was named by the Spanish colonists and means the Canyon of Saint James. The date is just before the end of World War II.

JULY 20

This section describes the reunion of Francisco and his grandson, Abel, who is a returning veteran of World War II. The section opens with a descriptive passage in present tense, suggesting the eternal beauty of the landscape. Then, moving into the past tense designating a specific event, the narration begins to follow Francisco. Riding his horse-drawn wagon from his home in the village of Walatowa to the bus stop, Francisco hums a traditional song. He pauses to check a snare he has set for a bird; the snare has caught a sparrow rather than one of the gaudier species he wants—a blue jay or a tanager—for a prayer plume. After discarding the sparrow and resetting the snare, he drives on. At a place called Seytokwa, the old man remembers a ceremonial race that he had run as a young man; he had beaten another runner named Mariano and had struck the exhausted Mariano away as he himself ran exuberantly into the central square of the village. Later, Francisco had recorded this race in a diary of words and pictures that he kept in a ledger book. He arrives at the bus stop, and his grandson, Abel, gets off. Abel is drunk and Francisco helps him into the wagon and sets out for home.

- **tamarack** a North American larch, of the pine family; the name is thought to be of Algonquian origin.
- **mesa** a flat steep-sided hill.
- *piñones* pine trees and the edible nuts harvested from them.

- **prayer plume**   an offering to the spirit(s) of a certain place, made by tying feathers to a specially painted and/or carved stick, reed, or other support. The making of prayer plumes is prescribed ritual, from the type of knots used to the words said when putting the offering together.

- *Sí, bien hecho*   Yes, it's well made (Spanish).

- *Yo heyana oh . . .*   chorus vocables from a traditional song.

- *Abelito*   diminutive form of "Abel" in Spanish, showing closeness, affection.

- *tarda mucho en venir*   a long time coming (Spanish).

- *Vallecitos*   literally, small valleys. Here, it is the name for a small lumber camp near Jemez.

- **Seytokwa**   an older settlement of the Jemez people, now uninhabited.

- *Se dió por vencido*   He gave up (Spanish).

- **the Middle**   the central plaza of the village.

- **ledger book**   a book ruled and lined to keep accounts. A number of Plains Indians of the nineteenth century used ledger books in which to record in pictures the history of important events in their tribe; for instance, there is a ledger book account of the battle at the Little Big Horn.

- **Cuba and Bloomfield road**   Cuba and Bloomfield are small New Mexico towns.

JULY 21

After sleeping off his liquor for a day and a night, Abel gets up early in the morning and climbs a hill that overlooks the city. The author follows this brief scene with six fragments marking milestones or significant elements from Abel's past. These brief stories are presented chronologically, from Abel's early childhood, when he was about five years old, to his recent experiences in the war. Some critics explain these passages as Abel's memories; they are presented by the omniscient narrator who tends to relate them through Abel's consciousness, but who sometimes steps outside Abel's vision for a more objective perspective.

The first episode relates an experience from Abel's childhood, when he was about five years old. Abel and his brother Vidal had gone on horseback to take part in the annual diversion of spring run-off to water the fields of the pueblo. This event traditionally combined religious ceremony, agricultural production, erosion control, and social festivities. Abel's mother was alive at this time, and she cooked for her sons and father; she died a few months after this event, and for a long time, Abel was unable to visit her grave.

Another event from Abel's early life is related in the second brief account. Once when Abel was herding sheep as a very young boy, he was frightened by a curse from an old woman who was drunk and had the reputation of being a witch. Running away from the old woman, he let the dog drive his sheep into the safety of a dry wash. However, the dog was frightened by the eerie sound of wind whistling through a hole in the rock. The sound filled the young boy with dread, and now the mourning sound of dread and anguish remains fixed in his emotional memory.

The third passage describes the death of Vidal, Abel's older brother. The child Abel had waited outside the house and watched the elders enter; then his grandfather brought him inside, leaving him alone for a few moments with his dying (or perhaps already-dead) brother. Abel spoke his brother's name.

The fourth episode takes place very early, while it is still dark, on New Year's Day in 1937, when Abel was seventeen, almost an adult. The narrator says that when his grandfather awakened him, he remembered shooting a doe in similar cold weather. Realizing that his grandfather had already hitched up the wagon, Abel finished dressing and joined his grandfather to participate in a ceremony in the nearby pueblo of Sia. This ceremony involves rituals performed by the clans of the village, by the crow, antelope, deer, and buffalo societies. After the ceremonies and some feasting and drinking, Abel and one of the daughters of the host had a sexual encounter outside the town, but the alcohol prevented Abel from feeling pleasure in the act.

The next episode that the narrator relates is much longer. It begins with a brief statement: Abel had seen an eagle flying with a snake in its talons, a portentous sight. The omniscient narrator then explains some of the history of the Eagle Watchers Society, one of the traditional clans or priestly societies of Walatowa. Members of this society were descended from a group of refugees, the remnants of a village called Bahkyula, who had suffered much at the hands of the warlike peoples of the Plains, as well as from disease. The refugees appeared in the early 1800s and were taken into the village of Walatowa. Poor as they were, they brought with them four sacred objects: a flute, bull and horse masks, and a statue of the Virgin Mary in her aspect as Queen of the Angels. In Abel's youth, the leader of the Bahkyush Eagle Watchers Society was a venerable man named Patiestewa. Members of the society have a reputation as seers and prophets; they are considered powerful in the all-important functions of rainmaking and eagle hunting.

After telling about the origins of the Eagle Watchers Society, the narrator describes how, by chance, Abel saw the eagle and snake. He was walking down a mountainside, returning from work for a rancher; looking at an awe-inspiring valley, he suddenly saw two golden eagles in a mating flight. The magnificent female carried a snake in her talons, let it go, and the male caught it in air, then let it go. The birds then flew away.

A few months later, it seems, Abel told Patiestewa what he had seen and asked to join the Eagle Watchers Society on their journey to capture live eagles for prayer plumes. Allowed to join, he set off with the other men. After making offerings and praying at sacred sites along the way, the men undertook a traditional rabbit hunt, killing or stunning the animals with small boomerang-like clubs. Abel took a rabbit and then prepared himself in the prescribed way by washing his head and gathering the items he would need to complete his eagle capture. Then he climbed alone to the remote eagle-hunt house, where he prepared a trap and waited near the rabbit carcass to capture the eagle. A male and female eagle approached the rabbit bait. When the female struck at the rabbit, Abel grabbed her legs and drew her into the trap. He then rejoined the group with his eagle; only one other man, San Juanito, had also caught an eagle, but it was an old bird. The men blessed this bird, talked to it, and set it free. That night, as the other men were eating, Abel opened the sack with his eagle, and, filled with disgust at the sight of the hooded, captured bird, he strangled it.

A sixth episode from Abel's past follows. This brief passage tells of Abel's departure for the army. His grandfather had not wanted him to go and was not present to say good-bye. This bus ride was Abel's first trip in a motor vehicle. He left the village and entered the life outside it, a life that would be filled with loneliness, confusion, and apprehension.

Another passage of recollection from the past follows. This final sequence opens with the narrator remarking that Abel suffers from a loss of memory about recent events. He can remember his past at Walatowa (presumably including the events narrated in the preceding paragraphs), but about what happened after his departure for the army, he can recall very little. However, he does remember lying on a battlefield among strewn leaves, bodies, and the wreckage of war. The constant din of battle had ceased, and in the silence, he heard the gathering sound of what eventually turned out to be a tank moving over the horizon and passing with deafening roar very close to him. The experience left him drained and shaken.

After these passages relating key events from Abel's past, the narration returns to Abel, at home in Jemez. It is morning and he is overlooking the village as the sun rises and the church bell begins ringing the morning Angelus. He is hung over, but responds to the bracing air as he watches a car in the distance approach and finally enter the village. He begins to walk back down into the village.

The omniscient narrator now shifts the scene to the house of the village priest, Father Olguin, who is moving slowly around his sacristy, getting ready to say Mass for the shuffling, coughing people on the other side of the wall. Two people are assisting at the service: old Francisco, Abel's grandfather, who acts as sacristan, and a young boy named Bonifacío, whom the priest sends out to light the candles, urging him to hurry. Then Father Olguin hears the sound of a car, which the reader knows is the one that Abel watched from above the village. A young woman comes into the church and is present at the service; afterwards, she visits the priest and introduces herself as Mrs. Martin St. John. In their conversation, the woman reveals that her home is in California and that she is staying at the Benevides house, some distance from the village, while she is treated at the nearby mineral baths. She asks the priest to help her find someone to chop firewood, and he promises to ask his sacristan.

Following this episode, the narration moves back to Abel and the late afternoon. His hangover has depressed him all day, but as he walks along the hilly outskirts of the village and sees the men working in the fields below, he feels comforted and at home.

- *cacique* The Spanish word translates as "chief"; it can mean boss, or as here, the head of a clan, or priestly society.

- **box canyon** a canyon with no outlet.

- **oven bread** bread baked in the characteristic beehive-shaped pueblo ovens that were introduced by the Spaniards; it is made from wheat and yeast. It is different from traditional cornbread that is baked on hot stones.

- **the crows and the buffalo and the singers came out** The passage refers to the dancers of the crow and buffalo religious societies as they emerge in their ceremonial regalia.

- **Navajo** The Navajo reservation is close to Jemez to the north and west of it.

- **Sia, Isleta** two other New Mexico pueblos, near Jemez.

- **arroyo** a dry wash, or creek bed.

- **Bahkyush** a person from the Tanoan village of Bahkyula.

- **mule doe** female mule deer.

- *kiva* The sacred place of esoteric ceremony and worship of the Pueblo peoples. Remains of prehistoric kivas in sites like Mesa Verde and Chaco Canyon show that they have traditionally been subterranean round chambers.

- **Domingos** people from the pueblo of Santo Domingo.

- **conchos** round, ornate silver disks usually fastened onto a leather strap for a belt.

- **Eagle Watchers Society** one of the clan, or priest societies, of Jemez pueblo; it is special because it comprises descendants of the Bahkyula refugees.

- **Tanoan** one of the Pueblo language groups; other groups are Keres, Tewa, and Towa.

- **Bahkyula** a village to the east, near the plains, from which the inhabitants fled and eventually settled in Jemez.

- *patrones* patrons, hosts (Spanish).

- **Pecos** a river in Texas to the south and east of Jemez. The Bahkyush people bring with them bull and horse masks acquired during their contact with Spanish missionaries; the masks will figure in the ceremony of Saint James (Santiago).

- **María de los Angeles . . . Porcingula** Our Lady of the Angels, from Porcingula. A Franciscan church near the town of Assisi, in Italy, is dedicated to the Virgin Mary with this title. The name was also given by Franciscan missionaries to the settlement in southern California now known as Los Angeles (the full name of the city is: Ciudad de Santa María Reina de los Angeles de Porcingula). The Bahkyush have a statue of the Virgin apparently acquired through contact with Franciscan missionaries.

- **Valle Grande** Great Valley.

- **a feast of martyrs** a day dedicated to a saint who was martyred. The priest wears red vestments to celebrate the Mass in honor of a martyr. However, July 21 is apparently not a martyr's feast, but the feast of a virgin, which would ordinarily require white vestments.

- **chasuble** the outermost vestment, often ornately decorated, worn by the priest saying Mass.

- **sacristy** the room off the sanctuary of a church where the priest puts on his robes and where things like hymn books, wine, and sacred vessels are stored.

- **cassock** the black or red full-length smock worn by priests and acolytes under ceremonial vestments or as ordinary dress.

- **Ándale, hombre!** Hurry up, man! (Spanish).

- **sacrament of communion** bread and wine said to be transformed into Christ's body and blood in the Mass.

- **Los Ojos** literally, in Spanish,"the eyes"; a place near Walatowa.

- **Mass** the central ceremony of the Catholic religion.

- *Bienvenido a la tierra del encanto* Welcome to the land of enchantment. "Land of Enchantment" is the motto of the state of New Mexico, and the phrase appears on road signs at the state's borders.

- **Benevides** The house where Angela St. John is staying seems to be named for Fray Benevides, a Spanish friar and explorer who wrote about his encounters with the people of the Rio Grande Valley in the 1600s.

- **sacristan** the man who takes care of the church sacristy, keeps it neat, locks and unlocks the church, and so on.

JULY 24

When this section opens, Abel has agreed to take the job cutting wood for Angela St. John. Upon meeting Abel, Angela is surprised and disconcerted that he does not bargain over wages. The chapter follows events from her point of view as she first watches Abel work, then attempts to communicate with him, and finally, after he leaves, brings in the wood that he has cut for her.

The narrator uses extremely sensuous language to describe Abel chopping wood; Angela's perception of his physical energy awakens erotic feelings in her which are tangled with some inner agony or conflict. She feels that Abel, too, is subject to inner hurt. The narrator also indicates that during the afternoons Angela feels a particular melancholy, which she seems to connect with the child she is carrying. Eventually, she goes outside to watch Abel finish his work. In their conversation, her pride is hurt when Abel still seems unconcerned about payment, and his silence irritates her. She imagines a sexual encounter in racist terms.

Abel leaves. The narrator describes Angela's revulsion at physical life—in particular, with her own body and the fetus within her. Sometimes she wishes to die by fire. Finally, as night falls, she picks up the chopped wood, aware of every physical sensation from the touch of the axe handle to the sawdust chips under foot. She recalls seeing a hillside gutted by a forest fire and imagines the heat and violent energy of that fire.

Later in the evening, as she sits by the fire, Angela is visited by Father Olguin, who invites her to the feast of Santiago in the village next day. She agrees to come.

After the priest leaves, Angela sits by the fire and daydreams about the corn dance that she saw at the pueblo of Cochiti. She regards the dancers as visionaries who have seen a vision of pure nothingness, and she longs for this perception of nothingness as a cleansing or stabilizing experience; she also connects the dancers' attitude with Abel's concentration on the act of chopping wood. Finally, she assures herself that she can master Abel, and she feels at ease.

- **mules** ladies' backless lounging slippers.

- **sacramental violence** Sacraments are sacred rituals of the Catholic religion. Sacramental violence would be a sacred, holy violence.

- **feast of Santiago** Feast of Saint James ("Iago" is another form of "Diego," the Spanish equivalent of "James"). Saint James is the patron or guardian saint of Jemez pueblo, and the day dedicated to him, July 25, is celebrated with a big fiesta combining secular merrymaking with religious observances derived from both Catholic and indigenous traditions.

- **the corn dance at Cochiti**   Cochiti is another of the pueblos along the Rio Grande in New Mexico. One of the festivals marking the sacred agricultural cycle is a ceremony to ensure continuance of the corn crop.

JULY 25

This chapter takes place on the feast of Santiago, or Saint James. The narrator reflects primarily the point of view of Father Olguin, with some elements narrated from Angela's point of view.

The chapter opens with a folk tale about Santiago. The story is attributed to Father Olguin, but it is not clear whether the priest is telling the story to someone or has written it down. According to the story, Santiago is a knight disguised as a peasant and is riding south from the Rio Grande valley into Mexico. He accepts the hospitality of a poor couple, who kill their only rooster for his supper and give him their only bed. When he reaches a royal city, he wins the hand of one of the king's daughters in a tournament, but the king, angry that a peon should marry his daughter, plots against the knight. The old couple's rooster emerges from the saint's mouth, warns him of danger, and gives him a spur; Santiago then defeats his enemies with a magic sword. At the end of his journey back north (back to Jemez pueblo), Santiago sacrifices his horse and rooster; from the horse's blood have come the horse herds of the Pueblo people, and the rooster's blood and feathers have been transformed into all the cultivated plants and domestic animals that the people use.

Following the tale, the narrator describes the hot, still afternoon. As Father Olguin and Angela walk from the priest's house to the ceremonial plaza, they pass an elderly man solemnly combing his long hair. The priest stops to chat, and Angela moves forward, aware of the increasing volume of the drumming and the sound of people congregating, singing, and talking. She breathes in the pungent smells of the animals and plants of the village. Finally, Angela and Father Olguin reach the Middle, an ancient dance ground like a shallow dish at the center of the village, and wait for the ceremony. Angela becomes caught up in the sound of the drumming on a nearby rooftop; it sounds to her like thunder.

Some fifteen or sixteen mounted men and boys enter the Middle; Abel is one of them, but he is ill at ease and awkward. Another rider is an albino man, wearing small dark glasses and riding a spirited black horse. The mounted men line up and take turns riding past and trying to grab a rooster that has been partially buried in sand. Abel fails, and Angela, watching, silently scorns his attempt; she is nearly overcome by the sensuous event, but smiles deceptively at Abel as he passes.

The albino succeeds in grabbing the rooster. He rides back to the men, pausing briefly in front of Angela, where she takes note of his consummate ugliness. Back with the other men, he carefully decides upon Abel for part of the ceremonial game. The albino then stations his horse so skillfully that Abel has no choice: he must passively submit to being the albino's blood-lashed victim. The albino beats Abel with the rooster until it dies and its remains are scattered on the ground. Afterward, women complete the sacrifice by throwing water on the fragments. Angela is drained by the sensory and emotional extremes that she has experienced; the narrator compares her feelings with her first experience of sex, which had also been associated with sacrifice and an emptying of feeling.

The narrator then begins to follow Father Olguin, who returns to his rectory, changes into an old pair of pants and sweatshirt, makes a pot of coffee, smokes a few cigarettes, and starts to page through a worn, handwritten leather book. It is the diary of a priest named Fray Nicolás and excerpts from this diary, from the years 1874, 1875, and 1888, follow in the text.

In the first entry, dated 16 November, Nicolás mentions his ill health: the symptoms appear to be of tuberculosis. He also reflects on the mischief of Viviano and Francisco, the altar boys who assist at services. Most of his diary entries are addressed to God. His language is reminiscent of early modern English, resembling the style of prose writers of the seventeenth century, like the colonial English diarists Samuel Sewall and Cotton Mather. The next entry, for 17 November, is a brief paraphrase of biblical verses. The following entry, for 19 November, mentions his worsening illness and a visit to a dying woman, Tomacita Fragua. The entry for 22 November describes funeral services for Tomacita, carried out with traditional offerings of pollen and feathers, a custom that the priest abhors. Later, the priest suffers debilitating symptoms and a nightmare. The entry for 12 December follows; it is only a couple of sentences commending Viviano and Francisco.

Another entry—this one written on Christmas Day—describes a Christmas Mass. Evidently the woodcarver who was to provide a statue of the infant Jesus did not complete his work, and an image of the Infant of Prague was used in its place. The priest names a number of people who took part in a living crèche, and then records that he gave the statue to a man named Domingo Gachupin to keep in his house for two weeks. As he is writing, he notes that he hears the drums and chanting of the Indian celebration.

One entry from 1875 follows, dated 5 January. Fray Nicolás first recalls celebrating the feast of the Circumcision (January 1) and then visiting the tiny settlement of Cuba, where he ministered to several persons. Returning to Jemez, he heard about the birth of an albino child; after visiting the family, he advised immediate baptism of the sickly looking infant. His own physical condition continues to deteriorate. After this passage, the narrator intervenes to explain that many of the following pages in the diary consist of sermons and religious texts.

Father Olguin then turns to a letter written by Fray Nicolás and dated 17 October, 1888. The text of the letter, addressed to Nicolás' brother J.M., first thanks the recipient for sending some books, then describes his worsening health, interspersing edifying comments on the inevitability of death. Then Nicolás complains that Francisco, his sacristan, continues to perform indigenous religious rites, which the priest regards as satanic. The priest is convinced that Francisco has impregnated a woman called Porcingula Pecos. The rambling letter then turns to an incident from Francisco's childhood, when he was hauled out of a freezing river and had to remain naked by the priest's fire while his clothes dried. The tone changes in the next paragraph as the priest complains querulously of his deprivations and mistreatment, suspecting his brother's wife of malicious gossiping about him. The last two paragraphs concentrate on his conviction of his closeness to God, stress his satisfaction in penitential suffering, and end with blessings for his brother.

After reading the letter, Father Olguin closes the book, satisfied to have vicariously participated in the holiness that he sees in Fray Nicolás. The narrator describes Olguin's inability to close his malformed eye.

The narration then returns to Angela's point of view. As she returns to the Benevides house, she sees it as part of the natural landscape; no longer a mere temporary stopping place, it will be, she believes, the scene of some secret exercise of her power.

- **peon**   peasant; fieldworker.

- **train**   a knight's retinue of squires, servants, and so on.

- **Pueblo people**   The Pueblo people are those Indians of the Rio Grande valley and other Southwestern sites who have traditionally lived in permanent villages of multi-story, multi-family condominium-type buildings constructed of adobe bricks, stone, and wood.

- **rectory**   the house of a priest or minister.

- **Middle**   the central ceremonial plaza of the village. The word also suggests the center of the world, as the Middle represents the place where, in the Native creation story, the first people, the Vigas, emerged from their journey up through the underground worlds.

- **white-skinned**   an albino. There is a relatively high incidence of albinism at Jemez pueblo.

- **centaur**   a creature of Greek mythology that has the head and torso of a man and the four legs and hind quarters of a horse.

- **chert**   a kind of quartz.

- **said his office**   the daily prayer prescribed for priests; the office changes each day in observance of the saint's feast and seasonal ceremonies.

- *Fray*   Spanish for "friar," a member of a mendicant, or begging, religious order.

- **soutane**   the black robe worn as an everyday uniform by Catholic priests at the time; it is often called a cassock.

- **María bear-HEE-nay et OMO FATUOUS**   A mispronunciation of the Latin "María Virgine et homo factus", which translates as "[Conceived by the Holy Ghost, born of the] Virgin Mary and made man." Fray Nicolás is characterized as punning in English, although presumably his diary is written in Spanish.

- **cassock**   a long black or red one-piece garment worn by priests and assistants at Mass, usually under a white pinafore, called a surplice.

- *Campo Santo*   "Sacred Ground," in Spanish; a cemetery.

- **War Captain**   a title belonging to the head of one of the traditional religious societies.

- **Nativity**   a religious name for Christmas, the feast of the birth or nativity of Jesus.

- *Sia*   one of the Pueblo nations near Jemez.

- **Don De Lay O**   a punning reference to the woodcarver who did not finish the statue of the infant Jesus on time.

- **Thy Mother**   Fray Nicolás refers to the statue of the Virgin Mary, which was completed by the woodcarver.

- **His Excellency's Conquistadora**   The reference is obscure. His Excellency could be the territorial governor (the diary is being written when New Mexico was a territory) or an earlier colonial governor. The Conquistadora probably refers to a statue of the Virgin. The "reconquest" of New Mexico by the Spanish after the Pueblo revolt of 1680 is celebrated annually with religious processions carrying statues of the Virgin and saints.

- **Blessed Infant of Prague**   Its origin shrouded in legend, it is a small wax statue of the infant Jesus, carried to Prague in the sixteenth century by a Spanish princess at her marriage. The original statue (as well as copies of it) can be dressed and undressed and has a rich wardrobe including jeweled crowns; it is venerated by many Catholics worldwide.

- **Epiphany**   a feast celebrated on January 6, commemorating the revelation of the infant Jesus to the three Magi, or Wise Men; it is also called Little Christmas.

- **Thy Patrons Little One**   Fray Nicolás is addressing the Infant, urging him to remember those devoted to him.

- **Circumcision**   On January 1, the Catholic church commemorates the circumcision of Jesus according to Jewish custom.

- **Cuba**   a small town near Jemez.

- *Tío*   the word means "uncle" in Spanish; evidently Fray Nicolás' horse is named Tío.

- **Lazarus**   The story of Lazarus and Dives is found in the New Testament; Lazarus, a beggar, is welcomed in heaven while the selfish rich man, Dives, is kept away.

- **Cor. I**   I Corinthians, one of the epistles of Saint Paul.

- **Sinister Angel**   a messenger or bringer of death.

- **Serpent**   According to Fray Nicolás, this is Satan, or the devil. Some kiva ceremonies, however, honor the plumed serpent that is associated with underground water sources and is believed to be a bringer of rain.

- **paten**   a small metal saucer that holds the wafer to be consecrated at Mass.

- **Host**   the consecrated wafer.

JULY 28

This chapter opens with several pages of lush descriptive writing, offering a picture of the landscape and its ancient, timeless character. The viewpoint is panoramic, panning across mountain, valley, and village below. The omniscient narrator describes various kinds of wildlife: birds—including road runners, quail and hawks—then snakes are mentioned; wild mammals like foxes, bobcats, mountain lions, and wolves are enumerated; and golden eagles, frogs, and lizards are also included in the catalogue. The narrator regards these wild creatures as superior to the later, domestic animals brought by Europeans: horses, sheep, dogs, and cats. The indigenous peoples have ancient rights to the land, having occupied it for 25,000 years—and their gods before them. The people are conservative; change does not appeal to or interest them, and they have maintained their essential identity and ancient customs even through the centuries long process of occupation by European/Christian newcomers.

After these descriptive and meditative paragraphs, the narrator follows Abel and his thoughts as he walks through the canyon above the plain. Abel reflects on his inability to reenter the life of the village; he is inarticulate in his native language and unable to communicate even with those closest to him. In the peaceful landscape of the canyon, he begins to feel more serene; he would like to compose a song honoring the creation of this extraordinary world. He passes abandoned settlements and the shaft of a copper mine and finds himself, early in the afternoon, approaching the Benevides house and the buildings belonging to the spa at the mineral springs.

The next few pages move to Angela Grace St. John's point of view as she hears Abel enter her gate and begin to work again at chopping her wood. She walks down to the spa and has a mineral bath; when she returns, she encounters Abel, who has completed his task. They go into the house, and Angela sets about completing a plan of seduction, but her plan is co-opted and she finds her emotions are very different from what she had predicted. After a brief conversation, she and Abel make love.

The remainder of the chapter moves to yet another point of view, a cornfield near the village where an old man is finishing an exhausting day of cultivating the plants. Not identified by name, the old man is apparently Francisco, as indicated by his lame leg. Underneath the rustling whispers of the corn leaves, he believes he hears a sound and realizes that some evil presence has been waiting in the field. Resigned to what life brings, the old man leaves the field after a brief prayer. As the irrigation water moves between the rows of plants, the narrator suggests that the alien, evil presence is the weak-eyed, eyelashless albino.

- **metate**   a mortar for grinding corn, seeds, chili peppers, and the like.

- **Tanoan**   one of the language groups of the Southwest.

- *Valle Grande*   Great Valley.

- **Torreon**   a city in Mexico.

- **Alesia**   a city in Gaul defended by Vercingetorix and conquered after a long siege by Caesar.

AUGUST 1

Father Olguin's point of view is presented at the beginning of this chapter. The priest is enjoying a deceptive feeling of oneness with the life of the village. Another ceremony is being prepared. This one draws many Navajo families and children; magnificently attired in velvets and silver, they enter the village precincts on wagons and prancing horses. Olguin fantasizes a self-satisfying visit to Angela, in which he will retain his officious dignity in spite of the erotic appeal she has for him; after ringing the bell for the noon prayer, he sets off to visit her.

Olguin's visit to Angela results in perverse disappointment. As a thunderstorm gathers in the mountains and begins moving toward the valley, he lectures her pedantically on the coming festival and the meaning of the various ceremonials. Aware of her own desire and its incongruity with the priest's fatuousness, she mocks him with the opening words to the Act of Contrition, a prayer said by penitents in confession. Angered and humiliated, the priest drives recklessly back to the village; although he almost hits a couple of children and narrowly misses colliding with a wagon, he can't shake his feelings of fear and repulsion. In the carnival atmosphere, he is reduced to a mere joke, and even babies laugh at him. While the priest struggles with his tempestuous feelings, the storm reaches the canyon and Angela's house; she welcomes it as a violent cleansing, leaving her with a previously elusive inner peace.

Meanwhile, within the village, the fiesta has begun. The narrator now follows a lame old man, again presumably Abel's grandfather, Francisco, dressed in ceremonial garb and shuffling from his home towards the kiva. As the old man smells the spicy, pungent odors of food, his reverie centers on the Navajos—the enticing aroma of their campfire cooking, the fellowship commemorated and renewed in this festival, and the desirability of a piece of Navajo turquoise jewelry. As he reaches the central plaza and prepares to enter the kiva, he anticipates the coming ceremony. The statue of the Virgin will preside over a ritual that is an amalgamation of agrarian fertility rites, signified by a bower of pine boughs and greenery, of Spanish commemorations of the expulsion of the Moors rendered in a mock battle with boys in blackface, and of a dramatic reenactment of the legend of Saint James. With great effort, he climbs the ladder and enters the kiva through the rooftop opening; inside is the compelling, overwhelming vibration of drumming and chanting.

With the other celebrants, the old man emerges from the kiva, and the pantomime drama of horse and bull takes place as the storm reaches the village. Both animals are portrayed by specially chosen dancers. The "horse" is a fine Arabian, and the dancer moves in aristocratic, high-strung steps, dancing among the clan priests and receiving their blessings. The "bull," in contrast, is a clumsy figure of fun chased by clowns. Francisco recalls having performed this part honorably several times in the past; he again remembers Mariano, whom he once bested in a ceremonial race.

The narration now moves to nightfall, after the ritual is concluded, and to a bar called Paco's, where Abel and the albino man are engaged in a murmured conversation, ignoring the inebriated Navajo men who have spent the afternoon there. The albino is described as an unnatural creature with an old woman's high unpleasant laugh and an evil mouth. Abel and the albino man leave and walk towards some vacant land across the highway and near a telephone pole. The narrator describes, in erotically charged language, how the white albino lifts his mighty arms to embrace Abel and how Abel draws a knife and stabs him repeatedly—just as the albino earlier lashed repeatedly upon Abel's body with the bloody rooster. The albino continues his macabre embrace of the young, angry man until he falls lifeless to the ground. The chapter ends by noting that Abel knelt for a long time over the corpse.

- - -

- **Mass** the main worship ceremony of the Catholic religion, in which bread and wine are believed to be transformed into the body and blood of Christ.

- **parish** the area and population which a given church serves.

- **druidic** pertaining to the druids, followers of a prehistoric nature worship in England and Ireland.

- **San Ysidro** a village in New Mexico, named for Saint Isidore, patron of farmers.

- **Dîné** Navajo word for "the people"; Navajos call themselves Dîné, not Navajo.

- **squaws, bucks** pejorative and insulting terms, used to describe those degraded by drink.

- **clansmen** Clan identity is of first importance to Navajos; naming and introductions always involve reciting maternal and paternal clans.

- **Angelus** a prayer to the Virgin recited at morning, noon, and dusk, signalled by the ringing of bells.

- **dervishes** devotees of certain Muslim religious societies, some associated with ecstatic practices such as whirling, howling, and the like.

- **Aesop** the legendary African teller of fables in ancient Greece.

- **Genesis** the first book of the Bible; it contains the Hebrew story of the creation of the world.

- **fabulous** exotic and strange, but also pertaining to a fable—that is, a story with a strong plot and clear moral message.

- **advents and passiontides** Preparation during the four weeks before Christmas (Advent) and the two weeks before Easter (passiontide) involves penance and discipline of fasting and prayer.

- **oracle** In Greek tradition, this person is a medium who carries messages from the gods; it can also be the message that is carried.

- **swaddle** a large diaper-like wrapping wound around an infant.

- *Padre*   Spanish for father; a title for a priest.

- **piki**   a corn bread made from fine thin batter baked on heated rocks into large, paper-thin rounds.

- **sotobalau**   yeast bread.

- **paste**   sweetened bread.

- **posole**   hominy stew.

- **squash blossoms**   The reference is to a necklace design consisting of a string of small, silver blossom-shaped beads on either side of a large central pendant.

- **Arabian**   an Arabian horse.

- **Moors**   Muslims from Morocco, rulers of Spain from the early Middle Ages until 1492.

AUGUST 2

This short chapter ends the first of the novel's four major sections. The celebration that began on the preceding day concludes with a procession, including both horse and bull, and the statue of the Virgin is carried back to the church. For the first time in his life, old Francisco leaves the village before the ceremony is over. He drives his wagon out to his cornfield, reversing the direction of his journey in the opening chapter, and he sees that the snare he had set for a blue jay has been sprung and is empty; the river rose and triggered it. As he begins to hoe, he can picture the dancers perfectly. He lovingly murmurs Abel's name and is aware of his profound solitude.

- **censer**   a gold or precious metal container for burning incense; swung on a chain.

- *Abelito*   "little Abel," an intimate nickname.

PART 2: THE PRIEST OF THE SUN

LOS ANGELES, 1952

As "The Longhair" is a title for Francisco, "The Priest of the Sun" designates Tosamah. In the two chapters of this section, Tosamah acts as a peyote priest and conducts a peyote ritual. However, his association with the sun draws more directly on older Kiowa tradition, which centered on reverence for the sun through the sacred sun dance and the figure of Tai-me, a holy image that, according to legend, came to the Kiowas as a gift from the sun.

The year is 1952, seven years after Abel's return to Walatowa and the murder of the albino. This part of the story will find Abel in Los Angeles after his release from prison, living among a group of other American Indians who have been displaced to urban locations by the policies of Relocation and Termination.

JANUARY 26

This long chapter opens with a brief paragraph describing grunion spawning at high tide along the southern California coast. In contrast to the correlation of images with seasonal events in the preceding section, this image is unrelated to the time of year, since grunion spawn at midsummer. The narrator emphasizes the helplessness of the tiny fish, an image that foreshadows what will be related concerning Abel. A detached, almost scientific voice narrates the passage. This omniscient narrative voice governs the chapter, but it moves in and out of individual points of view, notably Abel's, and, at one point, includes a first-person stream of consciousness passage.

After describing the small fish, the omniscient narrator moves to describe a storefront chapel called the Los Angeles Holiness Pan-Indian Rescue Mission. There is a notice that two sermons will be preached by Rev. J.B.B. Tosamah: "The Gospel According to John" will be preached on Saturday and "The Way to Rainy Mountain" will be preached on Sunday. The chapel itself is a squalid, dimly lit basement room with packing-crate furniture and a makeshift stage and curtain. When Tosamah appears, he is described as shaggy and cat-like, with a mixture of pride and suffering.

Tosamah begins his sermon with an elaboration on the opening phrase of the Gospel of John: "In the beginning was the Word." In a long monologue, he reflects on the power of language and the emptiness of a pre-verbal world, quoting from the Hebrew creation story: "And the earth was without form, and void; and darkness was upon the face of the deep." Then, along with a strange transformation in his tone of voice and appearance—from resonant, vibrant conviction to rasping, slumping indifference—his sermon changes and combines cynicism with reverence and awkward street language with high poetry.

Tosamah castigates the evangelist John and all his Christian followers for their corruption of language. Overuse of language cheapens it, he says, and people talk without meaning or thought, substituting invented ideas and nonsense for truth. Tosamah criticizes John for muddling and obfuscating with excessive references and digressions when Truth is actually profound and simple. It is assumed that the evangelist John was a white man, and Tosamah tells his congregation of Indians that they will be victims of the white man's manipulation of words unless they learn, like children, the power of the Word.

The reference to children reminds Tosamah of his Kiowa grandmother, and he mentions what a remarkable storyteller his illiterate grandmother was. He contrasts his grandmother's reverence for words and the sacredness of language with the multiplication and overproduction of language in the non-Indian world, which cheapens and pollutes language. Then Tosamah relates the story told him by his grandmother of the Tai-me: In a time of starvation, a man seeking food for his children hears a voice of thunder and lightning asking what he wants. He sees a being with deer's feet and covered with feathers. When the man explains that the Kiowas are hungry, the supernatural being—Tai-me—says that if he is taken with the Kiowas, he will give them whatever they want.

After telling this story, Tosamah returns to the theme of the Gospel of John, relating the origin and transmission of this story by word of mouth to the power of language to originate and make things happen. He again contrasts John's inability to come to terms with the power of language, which is older than silence, with the native appreciation for the power of language. As Tosamah appears to lose track of his thoughts, the narrator moves into his mind to describe a dizzying vision of sun, moon, and stars. Tosamah suddenly ends his sermon with the cynical advice to "get yours."

The omniscient narrator shifts abruptly to a question about why Abel should be thinking about fishes and the sea. Abel remembers his Navajo friend, Benally, talking about ceremonials that called upon natural wonders, but feels that Benally's frame of reference does not relate to the sea.

Another shift of perspective brings Abel into view as he wakes up, chilled, on a beach near what appear to be warehouses or a construction site. Recovering from a drinking binge, he realizes that he has been severely beaten and that his hands are broken. He remembers falling from a horse as a child and his back being treated by an old woman who served as the village chiropractor. He thinks back to his pleasure in his body and its strength and ability.

Two poetic lines allude to the sexual encounter between Angela and Abel. Next, a brief section relates Abel's jumbled memories of the murder of the albino, the corpse, and his trial six years earlier.

The next paragraphs move back in time to Abel's trial and open with a fragment of Father Olguin's testimony. The priest, as well as the court officials, are baffled by Abel's explanation of his actions: it fits no legal or moral frame of reference available to them. Abel recalls having lapsed into muteness after telling his story, convinced that he had done the right thing because in his eyes the white man he killed was his enemy.

In the next few pages, the narration suggests Abel's thought processes as he drifts in and out of delirium. He becomes aware of his surroundings, then moves back to a ceremonial run at the pueblo. Fragments of other texts are interspersed with the paragraphs that reproduce his memory. These text fragments derive from the society that surrounds the Indian world: the reader encounters odd snatches of employment forms, psychological tests, social worker questions. Abel recalls being on a bus going off to war and segues into a memory of a social worker, Milly, and their love affair, which he recollects in erotic detail. Milly is kind but naive. She believes in the clichés of the American Dream: a Second Chance, the Brotherhood of Man, Honor, Industry. Abel regains consciousness to hear the roaring of the sea, a sound which seems about to overcome him.

The narration then shifts abruptly back to Tosamah and the congregation about to begin a peyote ceremony. Tosamah begins by reciting scientific information about the peyote plant. Again, his language is a strange mixture of scientific precision and awkward slang; he has also painted his face in a striking, garish design. The ceremony is minutely described, including the altar, drum, and other accoutrements, as well as the contents of Tosamah's paraphernalia satchel (fan, drumstick, cigarette papers, sage), and the rolling of cigarettes and the blessing of incense. The central event of the service is the eating of peyote buttons. Following this communion, the participants drum, sing, and seem to ride a crest of overwhelming emotion. The prose suggests the ecstatic visions that the participants are having. The participants, including Ben Benally, volunteer spontaneous testimonials. At midnight, the effects of the drug begin to wear off. Tosamah goes into the street and blows four piercing blasts on an eagle-bone whistle.

The narration turns again to Abel. Fully awake and in pain, he recalls how his thumbs were bent back and popped out of their sockets. He is cold and shivering, flopping like the small fish described at the beginning of the chapter. The next section is a short paragraph recollecting an old woman called fat Josie, who comforted Abel with vulgar antics and coarse humor to distract him from grief at his mother's death. The single word "Milly?" intervenes in this reverie.

A section follows in which the voice of the omniscient narrator recounts the courtroom scene and the testimony of one of Abel's fellow soldiers regarding Abel's foolhardy courage under fire; Abel had stood up alone to a tank and appeared to do a kind of "war dance." Abel recalls resenting the soldier's presumptuous attempt to speak for another person. Again the single word "Milly?" interrupts the narration, which then returns to Abel and his mangled body. He lapses again into unconsciousness.

The next section replicates even more closely the confusion of Abel's thoughts. He recalls a duck hunt with Vidal, addressing his brother as if the two were together still. Thoughts of Milly return and become mixed up with the memory of the duck hunt; then, he remembers an afternoon of lovemaking and his concern to please her, both erotically and by getting a job. Another passage returns to the cold, fog, darkness, and pain he is experiencing, and then his mind drifts back to his initial sexual encounter with Milly at her house. Paragraphs set off in italicized type alternate with paragraphs in roman type for these passages, suggesting that the narration is moving inside Abel's consciousness in order to follow the troubled association of his thoughts. However, some of the italicized passages are themselves very poetic descriptions, reminiscent of the omniscient narrative voice at the beginning of this chapter, perhaps suggesting some vast, overwhelming sea of consciousness into which Abel's pain-wracked mind has been submerged.

Abel's memories then segue into a long first-person monologue spoken by Milly, in which she describes her childhood of grinding rural poverty and her father's hatred of the unyielding land, her brief marriage, and the death of her daughter, Carrie. It is not clear from the context whether Abel is represented as remembering Milly saying these things, or whether this is one more text inserted into this chapter, composed of a heterogeneous assortment of passages with different sources, points of view, and narrative strategies.

Finally Abel awakes and resolves to get help. He crawls into the back of a truck and rides for a while, then waits in shadows for other transportation. The cold and pain again drive him into unconsciousness as he imagines or sees Milly and Benally coming towards him.

- **A.A. Kaul Office Supply Company** the business that has a storage facility upstairs from Tosamah's chapel.

- **spawns** the silverfish are releasing their mass of eggs.

- **Priest of the Sun** a designation for Tosamah.

- *"In principio erat Verbum"* "In the beginning was the Word" (Latin).

- **Genesis** the first book of the Hebrew scriptures, source of the creation story.

- **Great Spirit** an expression non-Indians have used to allude to Native peoples' object of worship.

- **Jerusalem** the sacred city of the Hebrews.

- **Levites** in Hebrew tradition, members of the tribe of Levi; the priests responsible for worship.

- **Pharisees** in Hebrew tradition, members of a strictly observant group that followed written religious laws but also observed rules handed down through oral tradition.

- **Moses** the great lawmaker and visionary leader of the Hebrew people.

- **Philip, Andrew, Peter** apostles, followers of Jesus.

- **Kiowa** a people who migrated from the Yellowstone area to the southern Plains, noted for their horsemanship and bravery in war.

- **Tai-me** the sun dance image, called by Tosamah the sacred fetish of the Kiowa people.

- **"Beautyway"** the English name for one of the major Navajo ceremonials; these are extremely elaborate curing rituals involving hundreds of songs and prayers, body painting, sand painting, dancing, making sacred objects, and relating important stories. Their purpose is to cure disease—mental, moral, spiritual, or physical.

- **"Bright Path," "Path of Pollen"**   phrases that recur in many Navajo songs, signifying a proper, correct, enriching mode of behavior, the way for humans to move appropriately from youth to old age.

- **Orient**   Asia, the East.

- **fetish**   an object with spiritual or magic power.

- **Bull Durham**   a brand of tobacco sold in plugs for chewing or flakes for making hand-rolled cigarettes.

- **Sioux**   a family of languages spoken by the Dakota, Winnebago, and other Plains nations.

- **Algonquin**   Algonkian refers to a family of languages spoken by Cree, Ojibwa, and other peoples with homelands in the northeast woodlands. Bowker's use of this term shows his ignorance, as neither Abel nor any other character in the book is a speaker of any Algonkian language.

JANUARY 27

This chapter consists entirely of the second of Tosamah's two sermons. Much of the text was published earlier in a magazine article, and the whole chapter forms part of the prologue to the author's next book, an autobiographical journey titled *The Way to Rainy Mountain*. Tosamah is thus closely identified with Momaday himself.

Tosamah opens his sermon with a description of the landscape of his (and Momaday's) birthplace, Oklahoma. The language is richly evocative and poetic, recalling the earlier descriptions of the mesas, mountains, canyons, and plains around Walatowa pueblo. The prairie around the rise called Rainy Mountain is vast, isolate, sublime.

Tosamah/Momaday then begins to tell of his return to his grandmother's house for her funeral, and what he knows of this remarkable woman and the history she was part of. Named Aho, she was born at the last moment of glory of the Kiowas; Tosamah summarizes the end of that moment in the abandonment of the Kiowas on the Staked Plains, southwest of Amarillo, and their eventual surrender and transport to Fort Sill, Oklahoma, to be made wards of the government. Tosamah then moves further back into the traditional history of the Kiowas, from their emergence onto the northern prairie near Yellowstone through their acquisition of the horse, which gave them a mobility that made them nearly invincible rulers of the plains for a hundred years. Tosamah says that his grandmother carried within her a memory of places she had never been but was able to picture perfectly in her mind's eye; he determined to go north and recreate that migration southward, to recapture in spirit some of the glorious history of the Kiowa. He relates the Kiowas' migration to their origin story of having emerged from a hollow log: coming out of the forest onto the plains, they passed from darkness and enclosure into openness and light.

In prose that echoes closely the earlier description (in the chapter for July 28, 1945) of the plains beneath the New Mexico mesas, Tosamah describes the grandeur of the high plains descending from the northern Rockies. He describes coming suddenly upon Devil's Tower and being awestruck by this sublime natural wonder, then relates a Kiowa story of its origins. According to legend, seven sisters were playing with their brother on the prairie when the brother began to behave strangely and aggressively, and they saw that he was metamorphosing into a bear. They fled up a tree, and when the brother tried to climb after them the tree continued to grow until the sisters found haven in the sky. The tree petrified into Devil's Tower, and the girls remained in the sky as the seven stars of the Big Dipper constellation.

After another poetic, descriptive passage, Tosamah turns again to more recent history, relating that his grandmother was present at two final events: the last sun dance held in 1887, with the hide of a buffalo purchased—not hunted—in Texas, and the final incomplete observance of 1890, commemorated by the designation "Sun Dance When the Forked Poles Were Left Standing" and noted in the calendar by a figure of the unfinished lodge. Then the narrator moves to more personal childhood memories of his grandmother, recollecting in particular seeing her pray in a language unknown to him, but melancholy and moving in its cadences.

More poetic description follows, meditating on the lonely and picturesque character of isolated farmhouses on the plains. Then Tosamah returns to speak of his grandmother's house and the community of Kiowa elders that gathered there. He recalls the extravagant beauty and formal etiquette that characterized the people. The

- *House Made of Dawn* Genealogy
- Pertinent Maps
- Circular Journey Diagram

[possibly brothers]

(?)
(Porcingula Pecos) ≠ Grandfather Francisco   (Viviano)
[possibly Abel's
grandmother]

(mother) ≠ (father)
[unknown]

(Vidal)

Dr. Martin St. John = Angela St. John ≠ Abel ≠ Milly = Matt
[social
worker]

Peter   (Carrie)

```
( ) dead
≠ had an affair with
= married
⋮ spiritual mentorship
```

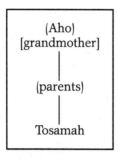

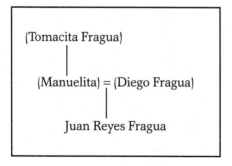

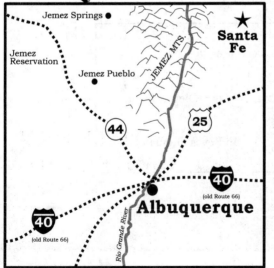

Jemez Pueblo is the setting for Parts 1 and 4. After Abel's mother and brother die, his grandfather Francisco raises him. Returning to the pueblo after a traumatic stint in WWII, Abel feels "at home" again.

Angela St. John visits the site for mineral bath treatments.

Highway 40 is old Route 66, the highway that Abel would likely take on his way from California to Jemez.

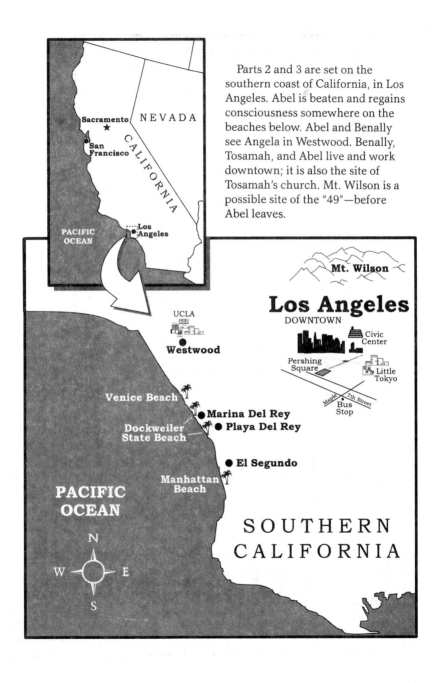

Parts 2 and 3 are set on the southern coast of California, in Los Angeles. Abel is beaten and regains consciousness somewhere on the beaches below. Abel and Benally see Angela in Westwood. Benally, Tosamah, and Abel live and work downtown; it is also the site of Tosamah's church. Mt. Wilson is a possible site of the "49"—before Abel leaves.

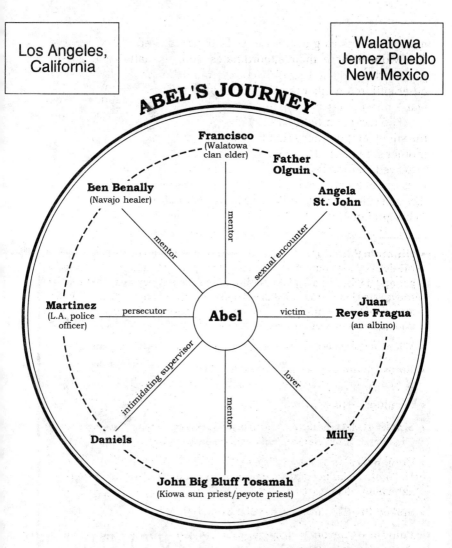

Los Angeles, California

Walatowa
Jemez Pueblo
New Mexico

ABEL'S JOURNEY

Francisco
(Walatowa
clan elder)

Father
Olguin

Ben Benally
(Navajo healer)

Angela
St. John

mentor

mentor

sexual encounter

Martinez
(L.A. police
officer)

persecutor

Abel

victim

Juan
Reyes Fragua
(an albino)

intimidating supervisor

mentor

lover

Daniels

Milly

John Big Bluff Tosamah
(Kiowa sun priest/peyote priest)

Circularity is important in both theme and structure of *House Made of Dawn*. Abel's return to Walatowa circles his life back to his home; the text recapitulates this circle, beginning with the homecoming race in the prologue and ending with preparation for that race at the close of Part 4. The journey from east to west and back again, however, is not simply one-directional circling, but involves backtracking and weaving in and out. It is comparable to a spider web, a potent symbol in Southwest American Indian culture of the creative force and harmony of the universe.

men he recalls as grave, wise, self-possessed, and full of reserve. The women were their subordinates, full of chatter and gossip, gaudily dressed and bountiful cooks. As a child, he would play with other children while the elders talked, prayed, and sang, and afterward, he would fall asleep near his grandmother.

The narration modulates to the present, as Tosamah describes the silent, empty rooms that he found upon his return for his grandmother's funeral. He carries the memory of a cricket that he observed, outlined within the circle of the full moon, and of the stillness of the great prairie night. His last comments tell of walking at dawn at the cemetery at Rainy Mountain to make his final farewell to his grandmother.

- **Hummingbird** a character in traditional mythology—especially in Mexico and the Southwest. Hummingbird plays a crucial role as messenger and adviser in a Pueblo myth relating the journey of the hero to retrieve rain clouds from a witch who has sequestered them. Hummingbird also figures in Southwest creation stories as a guide up through the underground worlds into the present world.

- **Wichita** a range of hills in southern Oklahoma/northern Texas.

- **Rainy Mountain** a center of Kiowa life and land in Oklahoma; the site of Momaday's (in the novel, Tosamah's) grandmother's house.

- **tornadic** tornado winds.

- **Smoky Hill; Canadian; Arkansas; Cimarron** rivers flowing through Oklahoma, Texas, Kansas, and adjacent areas.

- **Comanches** a southern Plains tribe in the Texas area; like the Kiowas and other Plains peoples, they maintained a nomadic way of life dependent mainly on buffalo.

- **Staked Plains** an area south and west of Amarillo, Texas.

- **Palo Duro Canyon** a deep, rugged canyon in northern Texas, called the Grand Canyon of Texas.

- **Fort Sill** one of many forts in the West erected during the campaigns against the Indians.

- **origin myth** a creation story; it can tell about the creation of the world or the origin of a clan or ceremony.

- **Black Hills** a region of South Dakota sacred to the Lakota/Dakota peoples.

- **Bighorn River**   a river on the northern plains in the Montana/Wyoming area.

- **Devil's Tower**   a monumental rock formation in Wyoming, upthrust through the flat prairie and flat on top; a sacred place to the Kiowas and site of one of their most important legends.

- **Big Dipper**   a constellation of seven stars, used in navigating to sight the North Star.

- **Blackfeet**   a nation of the northern plains, Canada and Montana.

- **Crows**   another northern nation, allied with the U.S. against the Lakota and Cheyenne during the Indian wars.

- **Washita**   a river winding through Kansas and Oklahoma.

- **Rainy Mountain Creek**   a stream running below Rainy Mountain.

- **Goodnight**   a ranch in Texas with a herd of buffalo.

- **Sun Dance When the Forked Poles Were Left Standing**   The sun dance was the central act of worship of the Kiowas—held once a year, when possible. The designation of this sun dance commemorates the fact that it was incomplete; the phrase would have explained an entry in the Kiowa calendar, a pictographic record of the tribe's history.

- **German silver**   an alloy of zinc, nickel, and copper.

PART 3: THE NIGHT CHANTER

LOS ANGELES, 1952

The title of the third part of *House Made of Dawn* designates the narrator, Ben Benally, a Navajo man who has been relocated from the rural, pastoral life of the northern Arizona/New Mexico Navajo reservation to the urban environment of Los Angeles. In traditional Navajo society, a chanter, or singer, is a person who knows one or more of the long, elaborate ceremonials that are held usually for the purpose of healing an individual from some spiritual, psychological, or physical disease. The chants, or "chantways," are religious rituals, and hence, Benally—like Tosamah and Francisco (and Father Olguin)—has a religious significance in the story of Abel's progress from sickness to health.

Navajo ceremonials are long and complex; some last as long as nine days. A chanter must memorize every detail—hundreds of lines

of song and prayer, designs for dry painting, dance steps and cos-
tumes, recipes for herbal teas and emetics, and construction of
sacred objects, like prayer wands. The Night Chant is one of the first
ceremonials to have been studied by non-Navajo scholars; it was first
translated and described by a military doctor and amateur anthropologist named Washington Matthews, who published a lengthy treatise
on it in 1902. This translation has been the basis for almost all further
study of the Night Chant and is the source of the phrase "house made
of dawn," which Momaday used for the title of this novel.

This section of the novel continues the story of Abel's life in Los
Angeles during the early months of 1952.

FEBRUARY 20

This is the longest single chapter of the novel; it is also unique
because it is narrated entirely by a first-person narrator: Ben
Benally. The narration is executed as an internal monologue, a sometimes dreamlike reverie, aided by a bottle of wine, in which Benally's mind wanders from his recent memories of Abel, Tosamah,
Milly, and Angela back to his childhood and youth on the reservation, and forward again to his life in Los Angeles.

Benally opens his monologue by saying that "he" left on this day,
and the reader soon infers that Benally is talking about Abel. The
two men had walked in the rain to the train station. Benally's reference to Abel's bandaged hands recalls the events of the previous
month and Abel's awakening, described in the preceding section, on
the beach after a severe beating, with his hands broken. Benally
then goes on to recollect walking home from the train station in the
rainy dark. His description of the traffic, lights, and motion of the
urban landscape is simple but poetic. Throughout this section of the
novel, the sound, smell, and feel of rain will signal Benally's
thoughts returning to his immediate situation in Los Angeles—from
his daydreams of life with Abel and, further back, his childhood and
youth on the reservation. At this point, Benally's mind moves back
to Abel and his worry that no one on the train will assist Abel, who
is still badly wounded, bruised, and in pain from his beating. He
admits to a feeling of loneliness among the strangers of the city.

Benally then describes entering Henry's, a bar typical of those
found among Indian populations of big cities. Benally recalls that a
vicious, hot-tempered policeman named Martinez sometimes comes

into this bar. He also notes that people call Martinez a *culebra*; this epithet links the corrupt police officer with the nearly blind albino whom Abel had murdered, and who was reputed to be a *culebra*. Benally sees a friend, Manygoats, whom he asks for repayment of a loan; Benally would like to stay and tease Manygoats and the buxom woman whom he is with, but he has pretended to have a prior engagement and so he must go. Reluctantly leaving what he perceives as the relaxed, friendly atmosphere of the bar, he goes out once again into the rain.

Arriving at his lightless apartment, Benally discovers that he and Abel, distracted by trying to entice a pigeon into the room, had left the window open, and, now, rain has soaked into the floor. As the radiator heats up, Benally continues musing on Abel's departure. He misses Milly, who had brought some snacks for Abel to take with him, and his reminiscences turn to Milly's evolving relationship with Abel. At first, she had insisted on completing paperwork for the social services agency, but gradually, she had come simply to socialize with Benally and Abel.

Benally's thoughts then turn to the preceding night. He, Abel, Tosamah, and Cruz had gone out to a "49" in the hills east of the city. Everybody got a little drunk. Benally recalls the drum music, the singing, the dancing, and the general conviviality, as well as the beauty of the night sky and the sparsely inhabited terrain. He and Abel walked off apart from the group of revelers to talk about meeting again some day; both plan to return to their homelands and, eventually, prepare a special reunion.

By a process of association, Benally's train of thought moves from his anticipated reunion with Abel to memories of his home and to the kind of appreciation he tried to convey to Abel. He ruminates on how he had told Abel about the sacred chants of the Navajos, and, at the party, he had begun to sing very softly a song from a traditional ceremony.

At this point, there is inserted into the narration the text of a translation of a Navajo prayer. This translation is the source of the novel's title: the opening lines invoke a sacred place, the House Made of Dawn. The whole text reads like a stately, free-verse poem in English, and it is extremely rich in its allusions to many symbolic and sacred areas of Navajo life. The most important of these concepts is that of "beauty," which is expressed in the chorus-like finale of the text. "Beauty" is the frequent translation of a Navajo word that encompasses the meanings "long life," "motion through time," and "balance." "Beauty" represents the appropriate centering of the individual within an ordered universe. Benally represents himself as singing this song for Abel. This is both an appropriate gesture and a critical turning point in the plot, as the song is a healing song, sung to assist a person in becoming cured from some illness or injury, and Abel is finally commencing a process of healing from his deep-seated malaise.

Benally abruptly returns to his memories with a comment that Abel was unlucky, and he recalls that Tosamah had called Abel a "longhair." The next paragraphs then center on Tosamah, as Benally recalls a conversation in which Tosamah expressed his delight at the astonishment of non-Indian society when confronted by a person like Abel. Tosamah's words were filled with sarcasm at the so-called "civilized" society's inability to fathom a person of faith such as Abel. He imagined with relish the confusion and incomprehension surrounding Abel's defense in court, a defense based on Abel's belief that the man he killed was a witch. The last remarks that Benally recalls are a prophecy filled with bitterness towards Christianity, which for Tosamah, represents the whole colonial enterprise.

Benally characterizes Tosamah's speech as crazy and asserts that the Kiowa does not understand Abel. It is different, he thinks, for people who grow up on the sparsely settled reservation than for those who have always lived in cities. In the vast spaces and harsh environment, all kinds of phenomena may be seen as supernatural, and it is easy to believe that a person who appears to have special attributes might be a witch.

Benally's memory returns to Abel's first day on the job in a factory, where the two of them worked on an assembly line stapling cartons. The day had gone successfully, in spite of Benally's apprehension that Abel would not tolerate the racist comments of co-workers and bosses. That evening, Benally, finding that the Relocation officer responsible for finding Abel housing had failed to do so, invited Abel to his apartment; this was the beginning of their friendship.

A brief section then summarizes Benally's relationship with Abel. Benally recalls especially his commonality with Abel: both are from reservations, and Benally can therefore sense how lonely

Abel must be. These two paragraphs form a transition to an extended reverie as Benally's mind travels back to his childhood.

In several pages set off typographically by italics, Benally recollects the peaceful, pastoral life of his childhood, surrounded by family, domestic animals, and the familiar closeness of life in the hogan. The style in these passages is fluid and affected, somewhat in the manner of Hemingway; it is characterized by strings of simple clauses joined by "and," conveying the sense of a vivid, almost hypnotic daydream. Benally's stream of thought carries him back to winter days in the hogan with snow outside, the smells of coffee, mutton cooking, and, outside, the clean crispness of the winter air. The prose also recaptures some of the wonder of childhood, when the entire world is open to the process of discovery.

Benally returns abruptly from his reverie of childhood to his more recent memories of Abel, and the downward turn of Abel's life in Los Angeles. Besides the monotony and meaninglessness of his job, Abel had had to contend with bossy, intrusive social workers, probation officers, and supervisors at work. Benally recollects also his own feelings of helplessness at his inability to assist Abel. A downward spiral had ensued, with friction at work, irritability with friends, and finally loss of the job. There had been a falling out with Tosamah and Cruz, an episode of drunkenness, and harassment by his supervisor at work. Events culminated in Abel's walking off the job. A period of aimlessness and apathy had followed, a few jobs held for a few days, and frequent episodes of drunkenness.

According to Benally, the few good times during this period involved Milly—picnics at the beach and simple, friendly socializing. Thoughts of Milly lead to musings on her life—a hard, impoverished childhood and the sorrow of watching a kind, gentle father unable to wrest a living from his unproductive farm. These recollections of Milly begin to produce associations with a girl from Benally's youth, and italicized passages of stream-of-consciousness reverie begin to alternate with the more proximate memories of Milly and Abel.

After a brief italicized passage, a few sentences recalling a place called Cornfields and the laughing eyes of a girl, Benally remembers sitting on the beach with Milly and Abel. The three are enjoying a rare moment of hope and simple pleasure. Milly has emerged dripping and sparkling from the surf, and Abel is moved to tell a story about a horse. The story is a joke—the horse had deposited a dignified elder in the middle of a river—and the three collapse in laughter at the thought of the pompous man's discomfiture. As Benally recalls Milly's laughter, he reflects that she was beautiful when she laughed, and once again, the memory of the beautiful girl at Cornfields intrudes. That girl had worn beautiful silver and turquoise jewelry, and the association with Abel's story continues in her name, Pony.

After a brief note that Abel's sickness could not be cured by finding a job and becoming assimilated, a long italicized passage relates Benally's recollection of a horse he had acquired many years before, a vibrant, exquisite creature. Benally returns briefly at this point to his room in Los Angeles, remarking on the rain coming down and, in his mind, tracing Abel's journey across the Navajo reservation in northern Arizona towards his home in New Mexico. As he pictures Abel traveling through his homeland, his mind turns again to the horse and the girl at Cornfields years before.

Another long italicized passage returns to Benally's stream of consciousness and includes another translated text. The passage continues the recollection of the memorable horse and the young man's joy in such a magnificent, well-formed creature. Being able to ride such a horse, he recalls, made him feel like praying, and the text then reproduces a song celebrating a horse. This song, like the earlier one, is rich in allusions to the mythology, geography, religion, and philosophy of the Navajo. It is represented as being spoken by one of the heroes of Navajo myth, the son of Turquoise Woman, and it associates the horse with the fruitfulness of the earth (corn, rain, rainbows) and with all kinds of good things (jewels, plumes, sheep, and the wealth of horses themselves).

Benally's reverie continues, as he recalls riding his beautiful horse to his grandfather's place, and his grandfather's joy at seeing him return. A festival was taking place, and again Benally recreates in his imagination the sensory details of the scent of wood smoke, the far-off compelling rhythm of drums, and finally, the sight of the beautiful girl who eventually became his dancing partner. It is a deeply romantic memory, a recollection of the girl's beauty, her shyness at first, and the tentative relationship that begins with the stately dance. The memory is preserved perfectly; no subsequent reality has returned to correct it. In the last sentence of the italicized passage, Benally reminds himself that he never saw the girl again.

The transition from this compelling reverie is abrupt: Benally returns to a specific event of brutality. One night, Martinez, the sadistic policeman, confronted Benally and Abel in a dark alley as they were walking home from Henry's bar. After shaking down Benally for his remaining money, the officer turned to Abel, who was empty-handed. The officer then struck Abel's hands with his flashlight, not breaking them but causing severe swelling and bruising. Benally recalls Abel brooding on the episode, as he had brooded in resentment at Tosamah's mockery. Abel's sullenness and passive-aggressive withdrawal had increased from this point.

Benally remembers another episode from this period: a trip to the western edge of the city and Abel's sighting of Angela. The two men had gone to deliver some merchandise from the carton factory, and while Benally was unloading the truck, Abel caught sight of Angela going into a department store. When she came out, he pointed her out to Benally, who had not believed at the time that Abel would be acquainted with such a woman. However, Benally recalls, he found out later he had been wrong: the woman had come to visit Abel in the hospital.

At this point, Benally's rambling train of thought returns to the apartment, the rain, and the old woman called "old Carlozini," who lives in the apartment below. He recollects a singular encounter with the elderly woman; her pet, a small rodent-like animal that she called Vincenzo, had died, and she had approached Abel and Benally. Unable to determine exactly what they could do for her, the two men had simply listened sympathetically to her disorganized, grief-stricken babbling. The memory causes Benally to comment briefly on the loneliness and alienation of the city, and he reflects that this elderly woman's only friend had been her pet. After the single encounter, there was no further contact between the old woman and the two men who were her neighbors.

Once again, Benally refers to the rain that has been coming down during this long night of memory and, it will soon turn out, drinking. In his mind, he defends the policies of Relocation and Termination, policies that Tosamah condemns. In contradiction to the richness and poetic beauty of the memories that he has just evoked of the reservation and his young life there, he asserts that the city is better. At this point Benally seems most naive, having bought into the materialistic promise of the so-called American dream, maintaining to himself that the ability to buy things is superior to the old ways of frugality and life close to the earth. Tosamah is wrong, he thinks, to criticize the efforts of the government to remove Indians from reservations and settle them in cities; he even begins to suspect that Tosamah may express his more outrageous ideas just to needle people. Suddenly his train of thought moves to the immediate situation, and he begins, it seems, to mutter to himself about the money that he had collected in the bar and how much he has left. It turns out that Benally had bought a bottle of wine, and his nightlong daydream and increasingly random reveries have been facilitated by consumption of the bottle's contents.

At this point, Benally's recollections of Abel turn to the last part of a rapid downward spiral: Abel's refusal even to pretend to look for work, more frequent bouts of drinking, and finally the fatal evening when Abel left in anger to find and seek revenge against the *culebra*—Martinez. Abel was gone for three days, then turned up at the apartment building—drunk, bloody, covered with vomit, and nearly unconscious. Abel's hands, in particular, were mangled almost beyond hope of repair. Benally remembers calling an ambulance for him and being forced to answer meaningless and irrelevant questions put to him by a hospital employee. Finally permitted to see Abel, Benally had feared that Abel would not recover. He remembers calling Angela, attempting to explain Abel's trouble and asking for her help.

Two days later, Angela visited Abel in the hospital. She chatted about her son, the child she was carrying when she and Abel had been together in New Mexico. She told a story that she liked to tell her son, about a young man who was the child of a woman and a bear and who grew up to be a hero and savior of his people. Benally is shocked that Angela has invented a story so similar to one of the most powerful Navajo myths, the story of Changing Bear Maiden.

After Benally's introduction of the Navajo Bear Maiden story, the narration includes a passage set off typographically with slightly smaller print; the font is similar to that used for printing Father Olguin's tale of Santiago and the two poetic translations from ceremonials. This text is a summary, as if heard from Benally's grandfather, of the story of Changing Bear Maiden. This maiden is one of fourteen children, twelve brothers and two sisters. The sisters survive a massacre and marry two men who, unknown to them, have been transformed from Bear and Snake. The elder marries the bear man, and when she realizes what she has done, she runs away to a mountaintop, where she eventually encounters the Yeí bichai, the Holy People, or semi-divinities of the Navajo religion. She gives birth to two children, a daughter and a son; the son eventually becomes a man of high position and weds the elder daughter of a chief. However, after he sleeps with his wife's younger sister, she has a child that she abandons; this child is, in turn, found by the bear. Benally's retelling of the story is followed by the last four lines of the House Made of Dawn prayer, invoking beauty all around the speaker.

Finally, Benally returns once again to his memory of the previous night, of the farewell party and his and Abel's compact to remember each other and meet again. Singing, praying, friendship, and drinking figure in his last imaging of a time that will be good.

- **Bunker Hill Avenue**   a steep hill in downtown Los Angeles. At the time of the novel, a funicular called Angel's Flight ran from the top of the hill to the street below.

- **The Silver Dollar**   a fictional bar in Los Angeles.

- *culebra*   the Spanish word for snake.

- **stomp dance, squaw dance**   social dances in which men and women participate.

- **Beautyway and Night Chant**   two of the great Navajo ceremonials.

- *Tsegihi*   Dawn's House, or the House of Dawn. It has been identified as an abandoned cliff dwelling along the northern Rio Grande.

- *corpus delicti*   literally, in Latin, "the body of the crime."

- **Jesus scheme**   Tosamah's sarcastic reference to Christianity.

- *What's-His-Name v. United States*   a fictitious court case title Tosamah uses for an example of the inability of law to deal with Abel's reasoning.

- **Kayenta, Lukachukai**   towns on the Navajo reservation.

- **Relocation officer**   a federal employee working for the Indian Relocation program. The officer was supposed to help Indians coming from the reservation to get job training, housing, and job placement.

- **firewater**   slang for hard liquor.

- **Indian Center**   Most big cities have Indian Centers, which are meant to serve the needs of people relocated to urban areas from the reservation.

- **Santa Fe Indian School**   one of the federal boarding schools set up for Indian children.

- **Wide Ruins**   a place on the Navajo reservation.

- **hogan**   the traditional Navajo home—a large, many-sided log building with a domed roof.

- **"greasers"**   a racist word for Mexicans.

- **Santa Monica**   a beach city a few miles west of Los Angeles.

- **Cornfields**   a place on the Navajo reservation.

- **corn-blossom necklace**   also called squash-blossom; a necklace of many small beads shaped to represent blossoms, with a large central pendant.

- *najahe*   the central pendant of a squash-blossom necklace, a design apparently based on the pomegranate.

- **Chambers**   a place on the Navajo reservation.

- *ketoh*   a type of tobacco smoke.

- **Williams and Flagstaff**   towns in northern Arizona, on Abel's route home to New Mexico.

- **Painted Desert**   an area north and east of Flagstaff, on the Navajo reservation; it is celebrated for its panoramas of multicolored rock and sand.

- **Klagetoh**   a place on the Navajo reservation.

- **Turquoise Woman**   one of the First People who took part in the creation and early shaping of the Navajo world. Her counterpart is White Shell Woman.

- **Belted Mountain**   a shortened form of Black-Belted Mountain; it has been identified by some scholars as one of the four sacred mountains that anchor the four corners of the Navajo world.

- **flexible goods**   one of the organizing categories in Navajo thought and language. Flexible, or "soft," goods can include items like leather or fabric, while hard goods can be turquoise or obsidian; however, assignment to a category does not necessarily depend on physical properties of hardness or softness.

- **Little Holy Wind**   Wind is one of the most important of the sacred elements in the Navajo world—it is the sacred breath of life.

- **Nambe**   a pueblo in northern New Mexico.

- **Apaches**   Like the Navajos, the Apaches speak a language belonging to the Athabascan linguistic family.

- **fried bread**   leavened bread that is fried in lard; it is characteristic of Navajo cuisine.

- **concho**   a round disk hammered out of silver (silver dollars used to be used) and strung on a belt, bridle, or other article.

- **Termination**   a program initiated by the federal government in the 1950s designed eventually to eliminate (terminate) all Indian reservations and assimilate all Indians into the mainstream culture.

- *Esdzáshash nadle*   "The Woman Who Became a Bear"—that is, Changing Bear Maiden, the central figure of the myth of the Mountain Chant.

- **Dzil quigi**   a mountain in the Navajo homeland.

- **Calendar Stone**   In meso-American cultures, the so-called calendar stones are huge stone disks carved with emblems of the sacred animals and plants, indicating seasonal and recurrent events and allusions to mythical personages.

- **Kin tqel**   a place in the Navajo homeland.

- **Yeí bichai**   Holy People; semi-divine beings who are figures in myth and song; they are depicted in sand paintings and portrayed in some ceremonials by dancers in costume and paint.

- **Mountain Chant**   like Beautyway and the Night Chant, it is one of the major ceremonials of Navajo religion.

- **Bear Maiden**   the heroine of an important Navajo myth.

- *Rio Mancos*   a river in the Four Corners area.

PART 4: THE DAWN RUNNER

WALATOWA, 1952

This last of the four major sections recalls the prologue and brings the story back to its starting point. The place is again Walatowa, and the year is 1952. The Dawn Runner of the title is Abel, who will now take his place with the other three men of traditional wisdom and custom in this novel: his grandfather Francisco, a Walatowa elder; Tosamah, the Kiowa Priest of the Sun; and Benally, the Navajo Night Chanter.

FEBRUARY 27

This chapter opens a week after Abel has returned to Walatowa and a month after his terrible beating in Los Angeles. The narration, in the voice of the omniscient narrator, picks up this part of the story at the point in the novel when we encountered Francisco in the first section—along the river. The poetic description here paints a midwinter scene, emphasizing the darkness of the water, the blanketing snow, and the lack of color in landscape and sky. The language evokes a world that is undifferentiated, silent and bare, lacking outline and definition. Like earlier chapters, this one is composed of short passages, which are set off by white space; they move across different time periods and points of view.

In the second of these brief sections, the narration moves to Father Olguin; he is at home in his rectory. The narrator describes the priest as having come to terms with his alienation and exclusion from the village and having arrived at a state of calm resignation and inner peace. His earlier eagerness has been tamed, and he believes the change has been brought about through his own efforts. The priest still occasionally consults the diary of his predecessor, Fray Nicolás.

The next section describes Abel as he watches beside the bedside of his dying grandfather. Abel has been faithful to this observance for most of the week, although he had gone out and got drunk after first arriving. As Abel sits by Francisco's bedside, the old man drifts in and out of a coma. Francisco talks and sings, but his speech becomes more and more disjointed—garbling English, Spanish, and Towan as he recalls random events from the past. His inclusion of the name "Mariano" and references to running suggest that the old man is remembering the same event that he had recalled in the first part of the book, his win over Mariano in the ceremonial dawn race. Listening to his grandfather in the small, dark room, Abel feels despair and confinement; he recalls that this is the room where he was born and where his mother and brother died. Abel is also in physical pain from his injuries and his drinking; all he is able to do is to make a fire to keep the chill off the room and to moisten his grandfather's dry mouth. He dozes throughout the night. Towards dawn of each morning, Francisco has spoken and Abel now hears the old man begin to speak in this dawn.

The next six sections appear to represent Francisco's six dawn speeches. However, the italicized sections are presented as stream of consciousness rather than as oral speech. Note that the narrator continues in third person as Francisco's stream of memories is represented.

In the first of the six sections, the old man remembers taking his grandsons at first light to the cemetery southwest of the village center. His purpose was to instruct the boys in the practical and sacred lore of traditional astronomy. He had pointed out the place where the sun rose at the solstice and also the sunrise points that marked the days for particular events; these events would include ceremonial dances, like the July festival that had been a tragic turning point in Abel's life, and the day for clearing the irrigation ditches in preparation for the spring rains. Francisco had spoken with care, aware of how fragile tradition is, how easily some small piece of knowledge may be lost forever. He wanted to be sure that his grandsons knew the importance of this knowledge that he was giving them, and that they felt the rhythms of the earth in their souls.

The second of Francisco's recollections moves further into the past. He remembers riding out as a young man and, after climbing a sheer cliff face, coming upon a cave with remains of the Anasazi, the ancient inhabitants of the Southwest. He had noted in particular a beautiful, thin-walled pottery bowl, miraculously intact despite the intervening centuries. His reverie continues with a ride on up the mountain, farther into a profound and vibrant wildness, where he takes note of the tracks of many different animals, and where the animals take note of him. He had made camp and was awakened by the agitation of his horses; his camp was encircled by wolves, who watched him with grave curiosity and wonder. The young man had raised his gun, then lowered it in salutation to the animals. It seems that he had been hunting a bear. With the dawn, he had continued tracking the bear, picking up its trail ever more clearly until finally, in a small clearing, he confronted the animal. He had shot the bear cleanly and quickly butchered the carcass, taking care to make the proper offerings. On the return trip, the young hunter had trained his colt to conquer fear of the bear's scent, riding it while the experienced hunting horse carried the bear's carcass. Upon his return to the village, he had been welcomed as a hunter come of age, sharing his bounty with the community.

The third of Francisco's reveries carries him back to an affair with a beautiful young woman. His lover appears to have been the daughter of the old Pecos woman who was referred to earlier in the book, named for her facial hair and suspected of being a witch. The dying man recollects in vivid specificity the details of their lovemaking. He also recalls that his lover had reminded him of his position as apprentice sacristan and of the rumor that he, Francisco, was the son of the village priest, Fray Nicolás. The woman had carried his child, increasing in beauty as her pregnancy progressed. However, the child was stillborn, and Francisco had turned away from the woman.

The fourth memory, like the first two, takes Francisco back to an event of dawn and sunrise. The brief passage relates how he had taken his grandsons, when they were still young children, to the edge of an overlook where, just as the sun rose, they could hear the sound of the dawn runners, the men running the race of the dead, the race that Abel is running at the beginning and end of the story.

Francisco's fifth memory, like the recollection of the bear hunt, brings to mind the successful completion of an action carried out according to ritual prescription and his passage into a place of new status in the community. He had been the drum bearer for the squash clan in one of the ceremonials. Apprehensive at first, conscious of the scrutiny of the people, he had soon lost himself in the hypnotic rhythms of the singing and drumming. At a certain point in the procession, he had to change to a new drum. The change had gone as smoothly as handing off the baton in a relay race, and the old man's memory lingers on the perfection of the moment and the admiration of the people. After that demonstration, he had been respected as a voice in the clan and had begun to be a healer.

The last of these recollections is very brief and ends the chapter. Francisco recalls a time when he ran foolishly, competing with a runner, going at the wrong pace instead of husbanding his strength. He reexperiences the sensation of bursting lungs and of continuing to run beyond the pain and exhaustion that he felt. There is the implication that this evocation of the sensation of shortness of breath corresponds with the old man's expiring breaths.

• **rectory**   a priest's house; it belongs to the church.

64

- *kethá ahme*   I'm a little bit of something (Jemez).
- *frío*   cold (Spanish).
- *se dío por . . . much, mucho frío*   It's very, very cold.
- *que blanco . . . diablo blanco*   how white . . . white devil (Spanish).
- *Sawish*   witch (Jemez).
- *y el hombre negro . . . muchos hombres negros . . . corriendo, corriendo . . . rápidamente*   and the black man . . . many black men . . . running, running . . . fast (Spanish).
- *yempah!* What are you doing? (Jemez).
- **igneous**   rock that has been molten.
- **peneplain**   land worn down by erosion.
- *Ándale, muchacho!*   Hurry up, boy! (Spanish).
- *Arroyo Bajo*   An arroyo is a dry wash or gully; Arroyo Bajo is a place name specific to Walatowa.
- *Vallecitos*   little valleys (Spanish); a place name in New Mexico.
- **scarlet pods**   dried red chili peppers hanging from the beams of the adobe houses.
- **squash clan**   one of the priestly societies charged with conducting ceremonials.
- **queue**   a single braid of hair.

FEBRUARY 28

This is the last chapter of the novel, and one of the shortest. Abel wakes suddenly some time before dawn. In the chill room, he senses a profound stillness and realizes that his grandfather is dead. By the light of the glowing embers, he prepares the body in the ritual manner, washing and braiding the hair and dressing the body in the old man's best clothes: a dark red velveteen shirt, white pants, and moccasins. He completes the appropriate offerings of pollen and meal and places significant objects—corn, feathers, and his grandfather's ledger book—alongside the body. Then, in the darkness, Abel walks to the rectory and awakens Father Olguin with the news that his grandfather is dead and that the priest must bury him. The priest is at first irritated and out of sorts at having been awakened too early, but as Abel disappears into the darkness, Father Olguin suddenly shouts after him the words "I understand!"

In the book's conclusion, the omniscient narrator follows Abel as he walks to the edge of town without returning to his grandfather's house. As the first light begins to wash over the landscape, he reaches a group of men huddled together, waiting upon the dawn. Suddenly, without warning, the men begin to run. After a startled moment, Abel runs with them. He runs through the snow on the ground and through a drizzling rain that has begun to fall. Out of condition, he falls and suffers from shortness of breath and pain in all his limbs. However, he keeps running, at first aware of the men ahead of him but then concentrated solely within himself, giving himself totally over to the act. This scene recapitulates the opening of the book, the prologue which described from a panoramic perspective high above the plain, Abel, a solitary figure, running through the dawn rain. At last, under his breath, he begins to sing. The book ends with Abel's song, lines from the Night Chant prayer that Benally had sung to him: house made of pollen, house made of dawn. As the novel opens with the traditional Jemez formula for opening a story, the final word ends the story with the traditional Jemez storytelling closure.

- **kaolin**   a fine white clay used in porcelain making, for medicine, and as a body paint.

- *Qtsedaba*   This closing formula signals the end of a story (Jemez).

CRITICAL ESSAYS

BACKGROUNDS

Pueblo Ceremonies

Major events in *House Made of Dawn* are tied to the seasonal ceremonies of the Pueblo agricultural year. Abel recollects an early sexual encounter that took place at a New Year's ceremonial dance, and his sickness of soul appears in his killing of the captured eagle during the Bahkyush Eagle Watchers ceremony, long before he went off to war. Angela attends the Cochiti corn dance, a fertility ritual which she, a pregnant woman, perceives as a nihilistic vision. At the end of the novel, Abel correctly carries out the rituals for burial of his grandfather, and his ability to undertake the dawn run that is a striking emblem throughout the book signifies his reintegration into the whole life of the community.

As has been noted, Pueblo ceremonial life is closely tied to the agricultural year, and, in particular, to the life cycle of corn. All of the traditional arts and sciences are interwoven in a total cosmogony that relates all elements of the universe—human, animal, plant, mineral—into a cohesive whole. Ceremonies and other activities are undertaken to maintain this integrated, holistic universe and community. For instance, in *House Made of Dawn,* one of Francisco's last memories is of taking his young grandsons to watch the sun come up over a particular point on the distant mountain ridge. This is a lesson in astronomy: the boys are to mark the point at which the sun will appear at the summer solstice, and also learn other points at which sunrise will mark days for the performance of specific activities. Prehistoric and historic records of Pueblo culture demonstrate a highly developed astronomy which was essential to maintaining the agricultural cycle. For instance, as is again noted in the novel's text, it is necessary to know when to construct the dikes that will divert seasonal rainwater onto the flood plain to irrigate the crops and control erosion. The day for doing this is indicated by another of the sunrise points on the mountain ridge that Francisco identifies for the boys.

The feast of Saint James, which is the occasion for the homicide that sends Abel into a second exile, exemplifies the separate and diverse elements in the observances of the pueblos. The people of Walatowa have included Christian saints and have enacted a secular European folk tale within the time prescribed for the realization of an indigenous ceremony, and they participate in both. This coincident participation in two separate ceremonies from two different and intact traditions is an example of *syncretism,* whereas the blending of Christian and Native traditions into a single, new worship in the peyote way constitutes a *synthesis.*

The Peyote Way

One of the religious traditions depicted in *House Made of Dawn* is the peyote religion. The peyote ritual presided over by Tosamah is the ceremonial expression of a religious movement that originated in north central Mexico, from where it spread northward through the southern plains and eventually became diffused throughout North America. In the course of adaptation to conditions in the United States, the peyote religion incorporated Christian elements. For instance, it is clear in *House Made of Dawn* that the ceremony is a communion ritual similar to other Christian communion services. The testimonials offered by each of the participants are reminiscent of the personal testimony of conversion or salvation, which is so important in some evangelical Protestant denominations. However, other elements such as the use of feathers and smoked herbs, the eagle-bone whistle, and the ingestion of the peyote—a mild hallucinogen found in a succulent plant native to Mexico—derive from Native traditions.

Historically, the peyote religion has been suspect to outsiders. Conservative tribal people opposed peyote worship because it superseded and threatened the continuance of traditional religious practice. Non-Indians were disturbed by the use of a hallucinogenic substance, in particular, and the expression of any "pagan" belief system, in general. The peyote religion of the Native American Church has been described as the first important pan-Indian movement, and early adherents sought to win converts to the peyote religion as an alternative to the pagan practices, which were not only under official attack from government policies but were also perceived as ineffectual in preventing alcoholism and family violence. Books like *Crashing Thunder* and *The Winnebago Indians* (both edited by Paul Radin) printed the testimony of Indians who believed that the peyote religion had helped them conquer dependence on alcohol and maintain family lives. Until a Supreme Court decision in the early 1990s permitted the states to restrict religious practices, the peyote ceremonies of the Native American Church received the same protection under the First Amendment as other religious services.

Navajo Chants

House Made of Dawn takes its title from a prayer that forms part of a long, extremely elaborate Navajo ritual, the Night Chant. This prayer, along with other texts and a volume of information about the Night Chant ceremony, was transcribed and edited during the 1890s by an army physician and self-trained anthropologist named Washington Matthews. Navajo chantways are not, like Pueblo agricultural ceremonies, tied to a seasonal cycle. They are specific for illnesses of various kinds, and how much of a given ceremony is performed for an individual may depend on several factors, including how much the patient's family can afford to pay. In *House Made of Dawn*, Abel is not treated with a full-fledged ceremonial performance, but is "sung over" informally and without public ceremony by Ben Benally; nevertheless, the power of the prayer's words is strong, returning at the healing moment of Abel's dawn run.

The need for Abel to have a ceremony is related to his status as a returning warrior. The figure of the warrior is central to much American Indian myth and storytelling. The warrior—and often warrior brothers or warrior twins—has an important place in traditional lore. *House Made of Dawn* emphasizes the unclean aspects of war-making: the pollution of mind and spirit that accompanies organized violence. Abel returns from war—drunk, alienated, and battered in spirit as he is later to be battered physically in the urban jungle of Los Angeles. Traditionally, a warrior needed to be cleansed and purified after his return home in order to keep the violence of combat from infecting the community and sometimes to neutralize or transform the power of the captured spoils. Certain Navajo ceremonials are carried out precisely for this purpose of purification after war; one of these is Blessingway, which some people say was in danger of dying out until after World War II, when so many returning veterans needed the ceremony that it was revived.

Benally mentions the Blessingway chant, but Momaday does not appear to draw on this ceremonial—which honors Changing Woman, the central figure of the Navajo pantheon—in *House Made of Dawn*. References to another chant, however, are implicit in the text. The Mountain Chant, also mentioned by Benally, centers on the story of Changing Bear Maiden. After he remembers hearing Angela's tale of a woman who had mated with a bear, Benally briefly recounts this story of a woman who embodies the mystical power and strength of the bear. On his deathbed, one of Francisco's significant memories is of a bear hunt. The power of bears and bear shamanism is documented in all the circumpolar cultures—Siberian, Alaskan Eskimo, Scandinavian and Germanic, Greenland, and Lapp, and its southward distribution is noted in China, Europe, and down to South

America. The governing myth of Mountainway, the story of Changing Bear Maiden, informs the references to bears and bear hunts as described and remembered by the characters in *House Made of Dawn*.

The two poetic translations incorporated into the text of *House Made of Dawn* are replete with references to specific elements of Navajo thought, myth, and tradition. In both texts, the balance of elements is essential. The first passage, from which the novel takes its title, emphasizes the balance of opposites throughout in its invocation of dawn/evening light, male rain/female rain, and so on. Male rain is sometimes characterized as a strong, pounding rain, and female rain as mist or standing water. Pollen and grasshoppers are part of the cycle of corn. Pollen is everywhere associated with growth, fruitfulness, new life, and holiness. Sprinkling pollen— whether corn pollen, cattail pollen, or pollen from other sources—is an integral part of many rituals. The prayer is sung as one of four honoring the presiding deities of the ceremonial. A "smoke" is referred to; according to the study by Washington Matthews, at certain points in the Night Chant ceremony a kind of cigarette is fashioned from a reed filled with tobacco and other herbs and smoked to cleanse the inner being of the patient. The invitation to the god suggests that the patient will be cured not merely of a specific ailment but will be restored throughout his body and, indeed, will be blessed with riches and long life.

The second poem refers to Turquoise Woman who, with her counterpart and sister, White Shell Woman, was one of the First People who fashioned the world at the dawn of creation. Belted Mountain may be one of the four sacred mountains in Navajo geography. These mountains are variously identified, although most identifications include Mount Taylor in New Mexico and the San Francisco peaks in northern Arizona. The mountains are alive; each is inhabited by an animating spirit, one of the gods or Holy People who also participated in the work of creation and who reappear in certain ceremonials to bless the people. Images like the rainbow, lightning, black clouds, and corn reappear in this poem also. Particularly significant is the rainbow, formed by the fusion of sunlight and water, which in Navajo philosophy serves as the bridge between heaven and earth, the pathway that is the correct and appropriate way of living for humans and their connection with the powers of the universe.

Benally also mentions Yeí bichai. These are the Holy People of Navajo religion. They include major deities like Talking God (also called Calling God), who figures importantly in the Nightway, and more recent additions to the pantheon who have less power and importance. Part of the realization of the Nightway ceremonial includes two representations of the Yeí bichai. Sand paintings are constructed depicting the Holy People; these paintings are considered to contain some of the power of the sacred personage, and the patient will enter the painting (thus destroying it) as part of the invocation to the spirits to enter and cleanse the patient. The Yeí bichai also take part, represented by dancers in costume and body paint, in the culminating dance of the final evening.

Witchcraft

Witchcraft is important to the plot of *House Made of Dawn*, although the theme is not explored in detail. Various scholars have documented how pervasive and strong is belief in witches throughout different cultures of the Southwest. Most studies of the phenomenon among Pueblo Indians stress that witchcraft is not inherent in any being, human or otherwise, but that it is a misuse of sacred power that is morally neutral. Witches are believed to be able to change into the shapes of animals, and it is their motivation that renders their activities evil. They seek selfish, personal gain or simply malicious destruction. Hence, witches can be "just anybody," as one person described them; they are not essentially or purely evil, but are individuals with near-supernatural power, which they use for bad ends.

Tosamah's commentary on Abel's trial indicates that Abel had believed that the albino could turn into a snake, and Benally, reflecting how belief in witchcraft is easy to understand in the context of the remote, mysterious landscape of the reservation, mentions the kinds of catastrophes attributed to witches—crop failure, death of children, and unexplained changes in weather. However, the albino in *House Made of Dawn* is not associated, by Abel or anyone else, with any disasters or even mishaps that might be attributed to malevolent intentions. The witchcraft that Abel attributes to the albino is one of the most enigmatic points in a very ambiguous text.

Federal Relocation Policy

The particular socio-political context of the two middle sections of *House Made of Dawn* is referred to by Tosamah and Benally, especially in Benally's recollections of Tosamah's objections to the policies. When Abel first appears at the carton factory, he has been brought there by a Relocation official who has failed to fulfill his responsibility of finding Abel a place to stay. The situation of Tosamah, Benally, Abel, and even Milly in the urban environment of Los Angeles is a product of the federal policies of Termination and Relocation, which were fostered especially during the 1950s and never really abandoned in spite of considerable evidence of their destructiveness and unworkability. The most accessible discussion of these policies is found in Vine Deloria's *Custer Died for Your Sins* (1988).

The federal programs were intended to be the culmination of assimilationist thinking initiated with the missionary efforts of Puritan immigrants. The intended result of the 1950s legislation was that Indian reservations would be abolished (terminated) and Indian people would be integrated into mainstream society and economy. This outcome would be accomplished largely by the relocation of Indians to urban areas and the provision of transition benefits such as job training and health care. As with other Indian programs, funding was never adequate for the benefits side of the program, and thousands of Indians found themselves in the slums and skid rows of inner cities—jobless, poor, and lacking the family and community supports that they might have turned to at home. It is just such a marginal inner-city environment in Los Angeles in which Tosamah, Benally and—for a while—Abel find themselves.

Tosamah and Benally manage accommodations to the new reality, Tosamah by following the model of the trickster and Benally by reliance on pastoral reverie. In his night-long reverie after Abel's departure, helped along by a bottle of wine, Benally defends the policy of Relocation in terms that show—in the light of events just described in the novel—a profoundly naive and sad acceptance of the shallow, materialistic values of the secular society. Benally criticizes what he sees as Tosamah's cynicism and nihilism (and indeed, on other issues such as witchcraft Tosamah does appear "not to understand"), but acquaintance with the actual outcome of Relocation policies would indicate that Tosamah's bitterness and despair flow from his perception of the irreparable damage accomplished by these misguided programs. However, Tosamah is also committed to his life and ministry in an urban setting.

The focus on Abel suggests another response to the historical pressure embodied in the Termination and Relocation programs: rejection of the whole scheme altogether, including the possibilities offered by Tosamah and Benally, and insistence on return to the conservative, traditional, pueblo reservation. Only when he rejects his urban career as a carton stapler and returns to his home place, reinserts himself into a way of life that values the sacred, and reconnects with the landscape and culture of his birth, can Abel's cure truly be accomplished.

VARIETIES OF NARRATIVE STRATEGY

House Made of Dawn is a complex novel which some readers find difficult to read because it does not follow a single chronological story line nor remain within a single consistent point of view. The seeming fragmentation and dislocation of the text is, of course, a deliberate choice on the part of the author, and it actually offers an indication of how the reader is to proceed. At the outset, it is important to recognize that the way the story is told is as much a part of the story—and of the act of reading it—as are such familiar elements as plot and character. *House Made of Dawn* challenges the reader to do more than follow (or "swallow") a plot: the reader must take an active part in the "construction" of the story, sorting and sifting through different kinds of texts related through varied points of view. The book presents a challenge similar to that of a puzzle, which must be pieced together from apparently random shapes in order for a coherent picture to emerge. In other words, the reader must pay attention to the writing itself, as well as to the story that is told in the writing.

Ambiguity and Instability

Many of the characters in *House Made of Dawn* are enigmatic and mysterious, although vividly realized. Their motives are frequently unfathomable. Readers often wonder, for instance, why Abel kills the albino: is it because he fears some personal injury? Or is he trying to rescue the community, as in the old folk tales, by eliminating an evil person? Is it revenge for being publicly battered and bloodied with the dead rooster? The albino himself is an enigma; he is never seen threatening anyone or in association with any evil that occurs in the village, yet Abel regards him, without question, as an enemy. The text does not answer the question of why the albino seems to go willingly with Abel out to the dunes: is he aware, as the text suggests, that he will meet his death?

Angela St. John is another mysterious character: is she simply a sinful temptation for Abel? How do the affair they have and the story she tells him much later, affect his healing process? What about Tosamah, who appears to make fun of everything, including the peyote that centers his worship?

The organization of the book, which seems to depend on a principle of fragmentation and reconstitution, also lends itself to gaps in plot development. One such significant gap is the question of who beats up Abel, breaks his hands, and leaves him on the beach. Benally recounts a scene in which the sadistic police officer, Martinez, bludgeons Abel's hands with a flashlight but does not break any bones, and Abel leaves the apartment days later with the announced intention of finding the *culebra* and presumably evening the score. Abel awakens on a beach, about fifteen miles from the inner city neighborhood where he lives, with his hands broken. Later, Abel turns up at the apartment, more dead than alive. Questions arise: was it Martinez who injured and nearly killed Abel? How did Abel manage to return to the apartment in his semi-conscious, mangled condition? This is one of several examples of the discontinuity of the plot, of significant elements that tend to disappear in the interstices of the patchwork narration.

With all of these questions, and others like them that emerge in the course of reading the book, the best approach may be to acknowledge and explore the ambiguities themselves rather than trying to resolve them. *House Made of Dawn* is a profoundly religious book, and the province of religion is the mysterious, the mystical, and the irrational. While religion may offer answers to the problems and questions of life, the answers are rarely reasonable and often seem wildly irrational. The following discussion covers seven textual strategies that Momaday employs in his novel; paying attention to these different types of narration and text can assist in an exploration of mystery and ambiguity.

Omniscient Narrator and Limited Point of View

The omniscient narrator is a detached, third-person voice that often tells the story from a panoramic point of view. The opening prologue of *House Made of Dawn* is an example of this type of narration, and throughout the book, the author tends to open chapters or sections with this scene-setting voice. This is the most authoritative storytelling voice, comparable to the narrative voice in oral tales and myths. There is no ambiguity regarding the reliability of the narrator with respect to events related.

The phrase "limited point of view" refers to an omniscient third-person narrator who, throughout a story or in part of it, relates the story as it is perceived by one or several characters. Many passages in *House Made of Dawn* are related from Abel's point of view. A crucial example is the scene—told in several separate fragments—in which Abel awakens on a beach after having endured a brutal beating. The narration follows Abel's consciousness as he tries to sort out the events in his life that have led him to this horrible situation. These particular passages exemplify the profound ambiguity of the novel, for it is here that Abel justifies his murder of the albino; however, it is also evident that Abel's thinking is distorted by pain as he drifts in and out of consciousness and loses awareness of time and his surroundings. The reader is required to ponder the question: what validity, if any, does the novel ask us to ascribe to the perception of witchcraft as a defense against the accusation of murder? Is Abel's judgment of the albino an expression of a culturally coherent set of values, or is it the product of distorted thinking?

Other episodes in the story are narrated in whole, or in part, through the points of view of Angela, Father Olguin, Francisco and Tosamah. In each case, the biases and personal agendas of the character must be taken into account as part of the storytelling. The text is destabilized as conflicting points of view subvert the reader's confidence in knowing what was supposed to have happened and how it is supposed to be judged.

Stream of Consciousness

Stream of consciousness is a narrative technique that was highly developed early in this century under the influence of psychological theories that focused on association of images as the foundation for mental processes. Stream of consciousness may be regarded as an extreme rendering of limited point of view, in which the focus of the narration is confined exclusively to the often erratic thought processes of a character's consciousness. This technique frequently includes distortion of time, disruption of chronological sequence, and general temporal uncertainty, all of which are characteristic of *House Made of Dawn*.

Reverie and daydream are terms also associated with stream of consciousness; they refer to a continuum of associational organization that ranges from examples like the lucid, self-contained memories of the dying Francisco to the gently inebriated ramblings of Benally, to the chaotic, disjointed fragments of consciousness of the wounded Abel. The reader can follow some of the stream of association in Benally's monologue as he recollects a horse story told by Abel, which suggests memory of a horse he once owned, which in turn recalls a girl named Pony, with whom he had a brief and sweet encounter. Stream of consciousness may be rendered through first-person or third-person narration, and *House Made of Dawn* incorporates both: first-person stream of consciousness occurs in passages narrated by Milly and Benally, and third-person stream of consciousness in passages narrated by a third-person narrator through the points of view of Abel and Francisco.

First-Person Narrator and Internal Monologue

First-person narration refers to a narrator who is a character in the text and who tells the story from the subjective, first-person, or "I" point of view. The third section of the novel, titled "The Night Chanter," is narrated by Ben Benally in the first person. Like narration from limited point of view, first-person narration can range from authoritative and reliable to destabilizing and unreliable. The possible biases, misunderstandings, agendas, and persuasive motives of the narrator must be taken into account. For instance, near the end of the section that he narrates, Benally criticizes Tosamah as utterly cynical and without understanding. This judgment must be read against Benally's consumption of a bottle of wine through the night and his naive acceptance of doctrines of consumption and materialism. Benally's section of the novel is represented as his internal monologue. There is no audience; Benally is talking to himself with the reader allowed, as it were, to eavesdrop on his daydream.

The second chapter of the section, titled "The Priest of the Sun," is also rendered as internal monologue, notwithstanding that it is announced on the signboard of his storefront church as the second of Tosamah's two sermons. This reverie is more focused than Benally's, almost expository in its development of related themes—and indeed, it reappears again as a single unit in the author's subsequent book, *The Way to Rainy Mountain*. Tosamah's second sermon challenges the reader to fathom the complexity of this character, whose nostalgic, deeply felt second sermon contrasts so poignantly with the cynicism and bitterness in the first.

Oration and Sermon

House Made of Dawn incorporates two formal sermons preached by Tosamah, the Priest of the Sun. The first, "The Gospel According to John," follows the conventional format of a Protestant sermon: a biblical text is announced, and the sermon then elaborates on its meaning and application. The text is the opening of the Gospel of John, and Tosamah uses the verse as a critical commentary on Christianity and the European civilization that supposedly embodies it. The sermon and Tosamah's language throughout this chapter are an awkward mix of serene lyricism, self-conscious pontification, and equally self-conscious street slang. This uneasy mixture again destabilizes the text, as Tosamah at times seems to be making fun of his own point of view and thus calling into question the seriousness of his critique. The two sermons also represent the novel's challenge to the reader to enter into the text and cooperate in "putting the story together." The first sermon is represented as preached to Tosamah's congregation during the peyote ceremony, but the second one is directed towards the reader.

Diary and Documentation

Written texts form a significant part of *House Made of Dawn*. Two examples of private, personal writing are important: Francisco's ledger book record of his life, and the diary of Fray Nicolás that Father Olguin pores over again and again. Francisco keeps a ledger book with figures denoting important events of the year. Such ledger books form an important subgenre of the art of nineteenth-century Indians, and Kiowa captives at Fort Marion produced a substantial body of work in this mode. Father Olguin, for his part, in the journal of his predecessor, Fray Nicolás finds references to people and events who appear to be part of Abel's history.

Another significant textual form in *House Made of Dawn* is what might best be termed bureaucratic documentation. Fragments that appear to be parts of psychological tests, employment forms, social worker paperwork, and court testimony are interspersed at crucial points in the narrative. Tosamah's first sermon, in which he excoriates the debasement of language that he finds in the white man's culture, offers a commentary on this verbal flotsam. Nevertheless, while often meaningless, the language of bureaucracy is powerful and can induce the kind of bitterness and despair that Tosamah occasionally expresses.

Folk Tale and Lyric Poem

Momaday incorporates several folk tales in the telling of *House Made of Dawn*. Early in the novel, the folk tale of Santiago and the rooster is offered as a recitation by Father Olguin. Another important story is the legend of the sisters pursued by a bear, which is retold as part of Tosamah's second sermon. The legend is part of the complex of images associated with bears and bear power. Benally becomes associated with the same thematic thread when he retells the tale of Changing Bear Maiden, after summarizing Angela's bear story. One function that these stories have, as do the poem texts, is to provide the reader with a mythic background and context for understanding the significance of the events in the story to the characters. A story based in European tradition might allude to Cinderella, for instance, or to angels; the author would not necessarily consider including explanatory material on these allusions because they are expected to be familiar to an American audience. Much, if not all, of the cultural context of traditional American Indian life will be unfamiliar to most potential readers, and an author writing from such a context must determine how much and what form of background assistance to provide the reader. Of course, the folk tales are primarily important as thematic developments of the story of Abel and the process of his healing journey that forms the core of the novel.

The two translations of Navajo texts are incorporated into the story intact as lyric poems complete in themselves. Navajo is an extremely complex language, and there is much debate over the extent to which these poems—torn from their ceremonial context and translated very cryptically—can be considered authentic representations of Navajo thought. What is evident is that both are English poems of great power. Their stately rhythms, rich imagery, and incantatory structure make them compelling pieces of literature. Moreover, the reader is invited, especially in view of Momaday's appropriation of a line from one of the poems, to regard *House Made of Dawn* as essentially a lyrical text—as much poem as story. This approach to the book requires a meditative, contemplative attitude—the same intense reading that would be required of a poem by Emily Dickinson or Wallace Stevens (both poets much admired by Momaday).

TOPICS FOR DISCUSSION AND WRITING

(1). Find (or draw) four pictures, one for each section, that would make appropriate introductory images for each section. Write a brief explanation of your choice for each.

(2). Silence has both positive and negative value in *House Made of Dawn*. Compare a passage or an instance of the positive quality of silence, and one showing silence as negative.

(3). What does this novel have to say about language? Consider what Tosamah has to say about language and its power, the passages excerpted from questionnaires and legal documents, and Benally's songs. What makes a given use of language benign or destructive?

(4). Momaday is a lyric poet and a painter. Analyze selected passages of description as poetic prose, attending to such elements as metaphor, simile, imagery, and so on.

(5). Setting and place are very important in this novel. Contrast the settings of Walatowa and Los Angeles, as described in the novel; how do descriptions portray the atmosphere and mood of these places?

(6). Religion is central to *House Made of Dawn*. Examine the depiction of, or references to, rituals from these religious traditions: Catholicism, traditional Pueblo religion, peyote religion, Navajo religion.

(7). Language is expressed in both speech and writing. Discuss examples of different kinds of writing in *House Made of Dawn* (for instance, Francisco keeps a diary or journal, and Father Olguin reads a diary written by a predecessor). How is writing used and misused?

(8). The title's emphasis on sunrise and dawn is elaborated in scenes and images throughout the book. Discuss images of sunrise and dawn and the importance of events that take place at this time of day.

(9). Storytelling has many functions in both literate and pre-literate cultures. Look at two stories that characters in this novel tell. Who tells each story? Who is the audience? Does the story reflect important themes in the novel as a whole? Does telling the story make a difference in what happens?

(10). The title of the novel refers to a house. What houses or dwelling places are described in the novel, and how do they relate to the book's major themes?

(11). The snake is a creature with ambiguous meaning in *House Made of Dawn*. Trace references to snakes in the novel to determine possible significance(s).

(12). If you are familiar with other fiction by American Indian writers, draw comparisons between Abel as returning warrior with figures like Tayo in Leslie Silko's *Ceremony* or Attis McCurtain in Louis Owens' *The Sharpest Sight*.

(13). Examine the anthropological literature on the Kiowa, Jemez, and Navajo peoples to learn more about the cultures Momaday refers to.

SELECTED BIBLIOGRAPHY

Books by N. Scott Momaday

House Made of Dawn. (1968)
The Way To Rainy Mountain. (1969)
The Gourd Dancer. (poems, 1976)
The Names. (1976)
The Ancient Child. (1989)
In the Presence of the Sun. (poems and short prose pieces, 1992)

Critical Works

ALLEN, FRANK. "Review." *Library Journal*, September 1, 1992, 175.

American Indian Quarterly. May 1978.

American Literature. January 1979.

American Poetry Review. July/August 1984.

Atlantic. January 1977.

Best Sellers. June 15, 1968, April 1977.

BODE, BARBARA, "Imagination Man," *New York Times Book Review.* May 14, 1993.

Commonweal. September 20, 1968.

Contemporary Novelists. 2nd Edition. St. Martin's, 1976.

Contemporary Literary Criticism. Volume 11. Detroit: Gale Research, 1974; Volume 19, 1981.

Critical Survey of Poetry. Magill Series. Salem Press, 1992.

EVERS, LAWRENCE J. "Words and Place: A Reading of *House Made of Dawn*" (211-230) and "The Killing of a New Mexican State Trooper: Ways of Telling an Historical Event" (246-261). Both in Andrew O. Wiget, *Critical Essays on Native American Literature*, Philadelphia: Hall, 1985. "Words and Place" offers a reading of the novel in the context of Momaday's sources, especially works on Jemez, Kiowa, and Navajo cultures; "The Killing" compares Momaday's fictional treatment of a historical event—the shooting of a highway patrolman—with short stories by Leslie Silko and Simon Ortiz based on the same event.

GRIDLEY, MARION E., ed. *Contemporary American Indian Leaders.* Dodd, 1972.

_____. *Indians of Today.* I.C.F.P., 1971.

Harper's. February 1977.

Listener. May 15, 1969.

MASON, KENNETH C. "Beautyway: The Poetry of N. Scott Momaday," *South Dakota Review*, 1980, 61–83.

Nation. August 5, 1968.

NELSON, ROBERT M. *Place and Vision: The Function of Landscape in Native American Fiction.* American Indian Studies, vol. 1. New York: Peter Lang, 1994. Nelson's is the most detailed study of Momaday's precision in locating elements of the story in specific places, particularly in the Jemez pueblo.

New Yorker. May 17, 1969.

New York Review of Books. February 3, 1977.

New York Times. June 3, 1970.

New York Times Book Review. June 9, 1968; March 6, 1977.

New York Times Magazine. March 17, 1985.

Observer. May 25, 1969.

"Review," *Publisher's Weekly*, September 21, 1992.

ROEMER, KENNETH M. *Approaches to Teaching N. Scott Momaday's "The Way To Rainy Mountain."* New York: MLA, 1988. This is mainly useful for the Tosamah section in *House Made of Dawn*, but also contains an excellent bibliography and list of other sources on Momaday generally.

Saturday Review. June 21, 1969.

SCARBERRY-GARCIA, SUSAN. *Landmarks of Healing: A Study of* House Made of Dawn. Albuquerque: University of New Mexico Press, 1990. This is the most extenSive discussion yet of the novel in the context of Momaday's use of traditional sources. Scarberry-Garcia relates the novel to the governing myths of several Navajo ceremonials and discusses Momaday's own use of anthropological sources.

SCHUBNELL, MATHIAS. *N. Scott Momaday: The Cultural and Literary Background*. Norman: University of Oklahoma Press, 1985. The most comprehensive general discussion of Momaday's work until the mid-eighties, this study also contains an excellent bibliography of Momaday's publications.

Sewanee Review. Summer 1977.

Something About the Author. Volume 48. Detroit: Gale Research, 1987.

South Dakota Review. Winter 1975–1976.

Southern Review. Winter 1970; January 1978; April 1978.

Southwest Review. Summer 1969; Spring 1978.

Spectator. May 23, 1969.

Times Literary Supplement. May 22, 1978.

TRIMBLE, MARTHA SCOTT. *N. Scott Momaday.* Boise, Idaho: Boise State College. 1973.

VELIE, ALAN R. *Four American Literary Masters.* Norman: University of Oklahoma Press. 1982.

Washington Post. November 21, 1969.

WOODARD, CHARLES L. *Ancestral Voice: Conversations with N. Scott Momaday.* Lincoln: University of Nebraska Press, 1989. Edited transcripts of leisurely conversations carried on over a period of years, this is a rich source for Momaday's sense of the writers, artists, and storytellers who have influenced him, how he relates to his ancestry, and his aesthetics.

NOTES

NOTES

NOTES

NOTES

NOTES

NOTES